THE ART OF
Skimming Stones

THE ART OF Skimming Stones

Leading Sustained Improvement in Schools

STEVEN TROTTER

Published in 2024 by Amba Press, Melbourne, Australia
www.ambapress.com.au

© Steven Trotter 2024

All rights reserved. No part of this book may be reproduced or transmitted in any form or by any means, electronic or mechanical, including photocopying, recording or by any information storage and retrieval system, without prior permission in writing from the publisher.

Cover design: Tess McCabe
Internal design: Amba Press
Editor: Andrew Campbell

ISBN: 9781923215108 (pbk)
ISBN: 9781923215115 (ebk)

A catalogue record for this book is available from the National Library of Australia.

Praise for *The Art of Skimming Stones*

"*The Art of Skimming Stones* is a wonderful journey through the growth of an experienced principal's approach to leading improvement and change. I love the SKIM Model; it shows a great balance of head and heart."

Tracey Ezard – speaker, author, educator

"Grounded in real-world expertise, this book provides educational leaders with practical insights and actionable strategies for leading meaningful change. It is an indispensable guide for those who want to work in deep partnership with their people."

Dr Simon Breakspear – author, founder, director, Strategic Schools

"As a former principal of 22 years, 46 years in education, now mentoring principals and coaching leadership teams, I have adopted many of Steven's ideas. The model is easy to adopt, empowers others, builds leadership capabilities, and improves student learning outcomes."

Deborah Patterson – author, leadership mentor, motivational speaker

"*The Art of Skimming Stones* is a valuable resource for leaders, providing a practical and strategic way of thinking about and planning for change. Steve's book is engaging and insightful, guaranteed to reignite a passion for leadership that is both motivating and energising."

Sue Richards – senior consultant, Growth Coaching International

"Steven Trotter has cleverly crafted a concise book that all school leaders will easily relate to, grounded in research and evidence from many well-respected sources. This book is a must read as it ignites passion to walk into the wind and have a crack to be the best person and leader you can be."

Nathan Owen – principal

"Once read, Steven's work will challenge its readers to reflect upon his vision and to provide a platform upon which to build a model of leadership which is clear and suitable for the needs of their current or future students."

Alana Moor – experienced educator, leader, mentor

I would like to dedicate this to my first educators and the team that encouraged me to take up various opportunities and inspired my leadership direction and opportunities: my mum, Kaye Trotter (1952–2022), and my dad, Peter Trotter. I have not thanked you both enough – my life experience, career, values, work ethic and personal attributes would not have been possible without your support and the committed way in which I was raised. Thank you both. I definitely know Mum will be reading and enjoying this book and looking down with pride.

I would also like to acknowledge the support of my family: my wife, Jessica, who is my best mate, my biggest fan, and someone who challenges me to think broadly and to see things from other perspectives. I may have written the words in this book, but it was a team effort, and I could not have done it without you. My children, Isabelle, Hamish and Ollie: you are little legends and motivate me to be the best person I can be every day.

Contents

About the author — xi
Acknowledgements — xiii
Author's note — xv

Part 1: Introduction — 1

Chapter 1 Setting the scene — 3
Chapter 2 What does skimming stones have to do with leadership? — 15
Chapter 3 Introducing the SKIM Model — 25
Chapter 4 Selecting the right skimming stone — 33
Chapter 5 Unload your cognitive load — 45

Part 2: The SKIM Model — 53

Chapter 6 Success — 55
Chapter 7 Knowledge — 67
Chapter 8 Inquisitive — 77
Chapter 9 Measured — 91
Chapter 10 The Meerkat Effect — 103

Part 3: Other considerations — 117

Chapter 11 Language is important — 119
Chapter 12 What if it doesn't work? — 129
Chapter 13 Research of influence — 139
Chapter 14 Conclusion — 153
References — 161

About the author

Steven Trotter has been a senior school leader and principal in a variety of school communities and settings of both small and large scale. Across rural, suburban and residential schools in both the primary and secondary education sectors. Steven has been a system leader as Network Executive Chair and an Executive member in two Victorian government principal networks. Over his journey he has built a passion for designing, trialling and refining adult learning architecture for educators and leaders to ensure we are on the path for sustained, ongoing improvement.

Acknowledgements

I would like to acknowledge the traditional owners of the land in which I live, lead and learn. The First Nations people of Australia were the first leaders, storytellers and educators on the lands where I experienced, developed, and continue to refine my educator and leadership capacities.

I would like to acknowledge the amazing support network I have had around me, particularly throughout the process of writing and editing this book. A small team of great leaders supported the direction and development of the early days of this book: Sue Richards (Senior Consultant – Growth Coaching International), Deb Patterson (Author, Mentor, Advisor with VPA, Leader), Alana Moor (Mentor, Leadership Coach, Leader). Your input, shared experience, and feedback was honest and valued.

There was a point in my leadership career where the flame had started to flicker out. I was feeling a little lost and out of energy. I was lucky enough to be appointed to a leadership position where my leader not only reignited my motivation and leadership energy, but turned it into a bonfire. Thank you, Jenny Crowle. I have never worked so hard, learnt so much, and felt so supported.

Author's note

All leadership examples are similar to actual events, but adapted to ensure confidentiality to anyone who was involved. Pseudonyms are used for staff names to guarantee that all examples are reflections of leadership actions, not individuals' experiences. Although the leadership processes and decisions are accurate, the narratives are intentionally modified in order to protect the confidentiality of any persons involved in my journey.

PART 1

Introduction

CHAPTER 1
Setting the scene

Leadership story of origin

Every human has a unique story of origin. What we sometimes fail to acknowledge is that this story of origin has a significant amount of influence on you, your values, your fears, your interests, your being. Whether it be family background or different experiences over your lifetime, these all add a small piece to the puzzle of how to do life. They are our reality, our perception, and how we construct our views of the world. These are neither right nor wrong, they are simply the small pebbles that build a riverbed. I can think of a family member who has a terrible fear of birds. As far as I know, they have never been savagely attacked or chased by a bird; however, something in their past (a story, a movie, a magpie) has caused this response. They are unable to explain why; maybe it does not make sense to you, but this has become a piece of their story of origin. It does not mean it is static – it can change – but it does mean that there is something underlying that needs to be addressed or acknowledged before being able to move beyond the challenge.

Now think about yourself: consider your story of origin. Why do you lead the way you lead? Why do some random things get under your skin more than they should? Why do you act in a particular manner when faced with a challenge? We should also consider that all of the people we are leading have their own story of origin. Maybe they have faced challenges from a previous experience that will cause negative or emotional responses that you or even sometimes they themselves cannot explain. Throughout this book, we will investigate how you can support and lead your staff through acknowledging individual differences as a reality. This is part of our work as leaders, which actually supports our work and makes us better leaders.

I can articulate a number of key moments that have impacted me throughout my official and unofficial leadership roles to date. I also know that there will be many more to come and many that I have not recognised as having a considerable influence. It is important to me to articulate and reflect on my experience so that I know what my default leadership positions are. If I feel like I am responding or leading in a particular way, why might that be? What has influenced that leadership decision. Ultimately, having this level of awareness empowers me to make balanced decisions, which are based on the people I am leading rather than skills, capabilities or values that are embedded in my personal leadership story of origin.

There are a number of core values and capabilities that underpin the SKIM Model and will be threaded through this book in various ways. Importantly, my leadership story of origin impacts my decisions and how I lead, as will yours.

Have you ever reflected on your individual story?
What is your leadership story of origin?

My journey has a lot of ordinary elements with a good sprinkle of hard work, taking some risks, and seeking various opportunities. My leadership pathway started at a young age, although I had no idea that was the path I was treading and that it would lead me to my different leadership experiences. I was an average student in primary school. I do not remember being a standout in any particular area; I was what I would consider "a bit of a cruiser". I started to branch out and have defined areas of strength as I got into high school, while also testing how far I could push the boundaries. I often think I would like to go back in time and walk into my high school staff room and say, "Hi teachers, Steven Trotter here. Just letting you know that in the future I am going to be a principal. I might even author a book or two." I can see my home room teacher, sitting next to my maths and

English teachers, spitting out their black coffee, with the cigarette falling from behind their ears in disbelief. I do not recall being a terrible student, but I do recall that my friends and I did not make life easy for our educators. My perceptions might be wrong. I feel their conversations would mimic my school reports and be along the lines of "Steven Trotter has a lot of potential, but I wish he would apply himself a little more".

Either way, I look back at that time of my education and reflect that I learnt a significant amount about myself. I was lucky: although my mates and I often acted like "turkeys", those mates are still my mates today and are all highly successful in their chosen professional fields, with beautiful families. So, we could not have been that far off the mark.

There are some significant parts of my journey that shaped my leadership to what it is today. As I reflect on my experiences, I do not believe in the polarising opinion that "you are a born a leader". I learnt the important values and skills of empathy, inclusion, work ethic, resilience, patience and persistence, among others. These were developed through experiences, failures, challenges, reflection and hard work and my parents modelling their expectations of me and my behaviour.

A big "peace" of me

My family were my first educators to whom I attribute my values and moral purpose. However, it was when these values or morals were challenged that I had to lean on skills that may not have been strengths to stretch my thinking. In early 1994, my best mate at the time invited me to a weekend camp called a "Mini Camp". I had no idea what it was or what its purpose was, but it sounded fun, and I could hang out with my best mate for the weekend, so I gave it a go!

At the conclusion of the weekend, the organisers asked if they could have a moment to speak to my parents. I remember Mum saying, "Oh no, what has he done?" They asked if I would be interested in representing Children's International Summer Villages (CISV) as an Australian delegate at what CISV called a "Village Program". This program was made up of 12 delegations of four 11-year-olds and one leader from 12 different countries around the world. The delegations met at a determined host country and spent four weeks in an intensive, fun, activity-based program where we learnt about each country, culture and religion. Most importantly, I learnt the importance of accepting others, both their and my differences and similarities, so we could connect on a human level without prejudice.

CISV started in the wake of World War II in the 1940s, when Dr Doris Allen developed a concept for an organisation that would foster inter-cultural understanding and friendship as an essential step towards world peace (see https://cisv.org/about-us/our-story/). Doris, an American psychologist, believed that by creating opportunities for children of different cultures, countries and religious beliefs to come together to learn and make friends, they would grow up to become ambassadors for a more just and peaceful world.

The 1950s saw the first CISV program, held in Cincinnati, USA, with the initial delegations attending from Austria, Britain, Denmark, France, Germany, Mexico, Norway, Sweden and USA. After the war, Doris intentionally selected children from these countries with a strong purpose to peacefully reunite children of those who had fought in the war. The signature program "The Village" was aimed at 11-year-olds, with Doris's research concluding that at the age of 11 you are old enough to leave home for a four-week program, but young enough to not have an embedded prejudice or misconceived cultural understandings and beliefs.

So, as an 11-year-old, with some sponsorship, fundraising and local government support, I left for Italy for my first experience of an international peace program with CISV. I loved the experience and pursued more and more experiences within the organisation. I attended many more programs until my early twenties, including an exchange to Indonesia as a 14-year-old, being selected as the only Australian delegate to attend a program in Costa Rica as a 16-year-old, and being accepted as the first junior staff member in this particular program's history. I attended the first "Summer Camp" peace programs held in Geelong and then the following year in Perth. One of my biggest highlights was being awarded a scholarship from the International Peace Fund to attend the Junior Asia Pacific Regional Conference (JASPARC) in the Philippines as an 18-year-old Australian ambassador.

Doris and her research outcomes were right: I learnt a level of tolerance, empathy and acceptance of difference in culture, beliefs and history. I had to lead with nothing short of unconditional open-mindedness. As a result, I have friends all over the world, but more importantly, I can dispute incorrect assumptions. I can think of many occasions when I have heard unjustified comments or beliefs about a race, culture or religion, particularly when there has been a significant world event. I can confidently say, "Well, I lived with someone from that culture or religion, and they are an amazing human being and a friend." CISV has a significant amount of claim on my leadership and my people-first focus. The intensity of these experiences is explained only through the experience itself. And like the students who walk through the gates of a school I lead, I implement my CISV learnings daily. These students will only be more advantaged by walking through my gates, stepping into that facility where they will be accepted based on themselves, their amazing and beautiful talents, and their own individual actions.

Running backwards to move forwards

As a young boy, I loved all sports and was OK at a few. In my mid-teens, a neighbour was umpiring local Aussie rules football (AFL) and encouraged me to give it a go. I eventually did so as a boundary umpire. The biggest motivation was that I was paid $20 a game. I came to love umpiring; however, this did not come without several hurdles along the way. I clearly remember when I first had to practise a skill that is important in general, but definitely in leadership, of being humble and respecting the decisions of those who were leading me. I had been training hard. I was doing well and getting great feedback from my peers in the time trials and skills nights.

There were some others my age umpiring whom I went to high school with, who spent a lot of their training mucking around or hiding around the back of the changing rooms having a cigarette. Game after game, they kept getting higher grade appointments than me, and over the course of the year I got a little frustrated, until one night I thought I would ask my coach why I was not getting any higher-grade games. Now I cannot remember what was going on at the time, but clearly, I did not "read the room". I approached the coach and asked directly, "Why am I not getting any higher games?" I clearly caught the coach on a rough night; he turned and (paraphrasing) said, "You are not good enough" (with a few other words to express how upset he was that I had asked this question).

As a 15-year-old, this was a big kick in the guts. I went home quite upset and probably would have thrown in the towel if Mum hadn't sat me down and given it to me straight. He was the coach, and I had a choice to either believe this or change his mind. So, Mum convinced me to get on the phone and apologise for questioning his appointments, and instead I set out to prove his opinion of me wrong, not through my words but through my actions.

The season ended and I had my "head down, bum up" approach engaged. I trained and came into pre-season ready to go. From there it was up and up. I ended up with a senior grand final the next season. After another two seasons and two more senior grand finals, I got my trial in the state league. The Victorian Football League (VFL) Umpires Association was another level again.

The strength of my character, making decisions calmly, quickly and fairly and following a process under extreme pressure and fatigue, has easily transferred into my leadership development. Particularly when faced with high-level issues or challenges, I refer to the process and meticulously follow it calmy and clearly.

I retired from umpiring in my mid-thirties with a good stretch of VFL seasons, double digits local league senior grand finals, a couple of opportunities to represent Victoria in National Carnivals, appointed to national Grand Finals, and named All Australian Country Umpire and Victorian Country Umpire of the year in one of the seasons. Umpiring has been one of my most rewarding vocations and among the most challenging experiences in my life. It put leadership into perspective. You need strong presence and process, with clarity and consistency. When that is implemented with regularity and with confidence, those you are leading (or umpiring) will grow in trust and respect towards you.

However, regardless of the decisions, it was how I behaved towards and talked to the players that often built respect on the field. Often a player would argue a decision. If I was confident in the decision, I would be assertive; if I thought I had possibly missed something or made an unwarranted decision, I would confidently admit, "I was blocked", "I did not see it that way" or "I may have been a little hot on the whistle on that one." Players did not run off saying "Thank you" or with a friendly smile – they were still frustrated – but I was always clear and honest with my performance. It was important to bring them into my calm when they were frustrated rather than joining them in their chaos.

This is like leadership in any organisation. When you are on the field in front of a crowd, you cannot hide behind a whistle. You must own every decision, whether right or wrong, and you build trust through honesty and fairness. We had the rules and process drilled into us weekly. As a result, the majority of the decisions were automatic responses to a process that was locked into my long-term memory (automation and memory will be discussed in Chapter 5, "Unload your cognitive load"). If you watch Australian Rules Football (AFL), the gap between the free kick and the umpire's decision, for example, is tiny, because the umpires are working on an instinctive process that is automatic. By having a process locked into your long-term memory, umpires (or leaders in pressure situations) – even when fatigued, sore, dehydrated or with a niggling injury – are more likely to make a correct decision because the process is automatic. The potential for human error remains; however, we need to accept that as a reality, admit the error, and work on the solution or next steps to minimise the risk of it happening again.

Talk the walk or walk the talk?

When I turned 18, I was fortunate enough to pick up a merchandiser role for Cadbury Schweppes. My job was to go to all the supermarkets and set up displays, help with restocking, and make friends with the managers. It was important to commit time to having a general "chin-wag" with the floor to store manager. They were the ones responsible for giving me better display positions than the competitors. As in all organisations, each manager was very different. I had to learn which ones loved to talk sports or gaming, which managers simply wanted me to come in and do the work, which manager did not really like me coming in at all, and which managers liked a freebie. I loved the challenge, particularly with the managers I found it hard to connect with. I would find new and adventurous ways to attempt to engage them. For example, the specials often started on a Monday, so on occasions where there was a big special starting, I would go into their store on a Sunday night to set up their display, so they walked in on Monday with one thing off their list. This strategy worked at times, but at others I may have set it up differently to how they wanted, in which case it backfired.

I continued to develop strong skills around engaging people with different expectations. I never expected them to change to connect with me – after all, I was coming into their workplace – I put the challenge spotlight directly on me and my strategies. I was the one who had to adjust or reflect on my approach to get the best options for the product and build a positive relationship, which was the vehicle for a constructive result.

I attended ACU (Australian Catholic University) for my teaching degree, and soon found myself on the students' association, then vice president of the association, and then president. As with my other leadership roles up until this point, I never reflected that I was leading and developing essential skills for my career and life. To me it was fun and exciting. I got to be involved in a lot of university life that many others did not. I attended conferences interstate and was invited to social events as a student representative, while also leading a lot of great events to engage our student population.

My grades at university did suffer a little as a result. I passed but I often had to "catch up". It was as a result of having to do extra work that I built up a dislike for missing deadlines. I had to focus on my organisational and time management skill development. By my fourth year, I had refined my processes to meet my work expectations, albeit not always at the highest level, but I ensured no deadline was missed. When I finished university, I remember thinking, "Wow, that was a fun ride. Lucky my learning is done and dusted." Boy, was I wrong!

Future maker or future breaker

One of the great quotes I heard from Muffy Hand (Muffy Hand and Associates P/L) was "As a leader or educator, you can be a future maker or future breaker". It was great motivation to have nothing but positive intent for the people you lead or support. I started my teaching career at a suburban primary school, teaching most levels over the years I was there. This was also where I got my first taste of school leadership. On occasions when my direct manager was out for a meeting or conference, I got the opportunity to be "Officer in Charge". I remember my first opportunity to take on this role. I was left with a list of approximately 10 low-level jobs to complete over the course of the day. Easy, I thought – until the first phone call, then the second, followed by a staff member calling me for support, a complaint about a bus issue, and a broken window – all before 10 am. It's fair to say I did not get one of the jobs on the list completed that day. I was a little stressed to hand the unmarked list back. When I did, my manager looked at the list with nothing crossed off, smiled, and said "Welcome to senior leadership."

In 2007, I applied for an opportunity to write a resource book for primary students and teachers for the Geelong Football Club (AFL). I was lucky enough to be successful, with five other educators. For the next four years (2007–2010), we planned, designed and published 3.5 student/teacher resource texts that got distributed for free to approximately 3000 teachers. The 0.5 of the 3.5 texts published represents a fourth text that was at the printing stage when funding was cut in 2010 so it never got published. This was an exciting opportunity to look at the intricacies of the football club and innovate a useful resource book to support the club's profile, linked to teaching and learning and the state curriculum. I still have copies on my bookshelf in my office: *School Cats* (Geelong Football Club, Digilearn, 2007–2010), for the one or two regular students who visit me and have a love of football. It's such a great resource to get them back into a positive frame of mind, engaging in learning on a topic they love.

Leadership is never a smooth ride, and I haven't always connected with all the leaders I have encountered in my different interests and roles over the years. Although at the time it can be significantly challenging, I look at these now as exceptional learning experiences. We know you learn more from being in a position of challenge than in a position of comfort, although both challenge and comfort have their own strengths and weaknesses in skill development.

Throughout my varied leadership experiences, there are only a handful of leaders who did not leave me feeling valued or respected as a fellow leader, educator or person. There was one particular experience that significantly impacted on my mental and physical health. At the time, I struggled day to day and had to find strength and validation in other spaces or through other people. I reflect on that time now; because of that experience I am a better leader and better person. I could not see the light at the end of the tunnel when I was in among the chaos, but now, having gone through that experience and others in both my professional and personal life, I know how it feels to be on the receiving end – not feeling the support or validation everyone needs in their personal and professional worlds. Therefore, I make a real, conscious effort not to have the people I lead feel as I did during those experiences. I remember how I felt when I was talked to in a particular way, ignored or belittled, either privately or in front of my peers. As Maya Angelou's famous quote puts it, "I've learned that people will forget what you said, people will forget what you did, but people will never forget how you made them feel" (Angelou, 1969). They are experiences I still reflect on and use as examples to coach my up-and-coming leaders today. They are also experiences that have influenced, framed and embedded the values that have helped shape the SKIM Model.

My education career has crossed over two decades, with my school leadership career spanning over fifteen of those years. I was a teacher-leader in a residential school where I got to innovate and develop a new program and curriculum from the ground up. It was here I learnt about the importance of culture and how positive culture can help an organisation thrive, while the opposite can dismantle staff efficacy without any warning. It was also during this period that I completed my Master of Education. My mini thesis focused on experiential education, with a particular lens on how residential education promotes friendship through the use of the outdoors (McDonough & Trotter, 2015).

Variety creates energy like rain creates puddles

In 2010, after a number of years living in regional Victoria (Australia), my family decided to move back to Geelong after our daughter was born. I was lucky enough to be appointed as a sub-school principal in one of the fastest growth corridors in Australia, Wyndham. I saw the school grow from roughly 160 students on its opening day to over 1500 in 3.5 years. It was a highly multicultural environment with a relentless focus on learning. This team of educators set the culture absorbed by an unwavering approach, focused on the importance of high expectations while not making excuses for our students: "They can't because… they won't because…" Every student deserves the very best education, and we were the school that was going to give it to them.

I do not think I have ever worked as hard in my life as I did at that school, but I also have never learnt as much as I did there. Although I did not have a "model" developed or a cool name, the SKIM Model had already started to take space and shape in my personal leadership framework and how I engaged and interacted with those around me.

Following this experience, I was appointed principal at a rural school in a beautiful little town outside of Geelong at a time when there had been several significant changes in leadership over the previous four years, and a level of disconnect from the local community. A retired principal, Doug, met me in the early days and gave me a piece of advice I have never forgotten: "Some of your best and hardest work will be at the front gate." Boy, he was right. I learnt a valuable lesson about the importance of community engagement. Having the odd sausage sizzle and chat at pick-up and drop-off is important and "nice" for relationship building. However, as I continue to learn, genuine community engagement in any educational setting has to benefit our most important clients, our students. Harnessing the local community's skills, strengths and passion to enhance the learning opportunities for everyone who walks through the gates is what I learnt was the true meaning of Doug's simple few words of advice.

From here, I slipped into an acting principal role for about 10 months to support another local school community before moving to a suburban school, where the community is so close they can hear the announcements over the speakers at recess. It was here that I learnt the importance of inclusion and defining what this important word looked and felt like in action. As a team, we started to define what that looked like and meant to our community – that being "inclusive" is as much about access to the curriculum as it is about extending and enriching the education of students at all levels of achievement.

I can honestly say that every school I have led or worked in has needed a different version of me. Every school has taught me a different lesson in leadership, a different lesson about myself and where my skills need to develop. The context is different, but I have always said – whether you are at a multicultural school in the fastest growth corridor in Australia, or a rural school surrounded by farmland – kids are kids, teachers are teachers, good teaching and learning is good teaching and learning, and great leadership is great leadership. Leadership research does not change when you change organisations, so the model I am presenting in this book will give you a starting point in any organisation. What you can then focus on is what leader does this organisation need me to be? What do the people (big and little people) I am leading need from me to reach their potential? The SKIM Model gives you the framework and space to focus on the people in your organisations while providing a great process to ensure the decisions you are making are supported with intentional leadership strategies.

Leadership reflection task

Have you ever reflected on your individual story?
What is your leadership story of origin?

- ☐ List the key events, experiences, roles and people that have influenced you as a leader. What skills, capabilities or attributes did you learn that built your leadership story of origin?
- ☐ What is your natural leadership default based on your leadership story of origin?
- ☐ Share this with your team.

CHAPTER 2

What does skimming stones have to do with leadership?

I was walking along a riverbank with my family during one of our favourite pastimes, camping. A beautiful flat stone caught my eye. I picked it up, wrapped my pointer and thumb around the sharp edges, waited for the breeze to drop so I had a flat surface, and then flung the stone low and flat at the water's edge. It hit the water and shot off, bouncing once, twice... and then in short succession three, four and five times – before sinking in the middle of the river.

My three kids were amazed, as if I had just revealed some sort of new dad superpower. They started excitedly picking up stones and throwing them at the water, but with little skim success. With my proud expert dad head wobble, I bent down and began the detailed, technical discussion of how to select the perfect stone, what is the most effective technique to ensure success of the skim, and finally, the importance of waiting for the right water and wind conditions before embarking on the throw. Our walk stalled, as my kids and I picked up and selectively dropped stones in the search for the perfect skimming stone. As we attempted "the skim", we discussed and reflected on our choice of stone, the timing of the conditions, and the technique we chose in our successful or failed attempts. After either a single splash or a skim off the water's surface, the stones eventually sank, but the excitement did not.

Before we get any further: if you are reading this and thinking, "I cannot wait to find out more about the best stone grip for skimming or the angle of impact required to get the best skimming result", I am sorry to disappoint you, but this is not the book for you.

However, if you are looking for a simple but highly effective framework to support your approach to intentional leadership in sustained improvement, then you are in the right place.

Where to begin?

The world of educational leadership is complex, and there is an enormous amount of research and articles supporting how best to lead improvement in any organisation or environment. It is wise for any leader to investigate the multitude of leadership frameworks already published. All models have benefits and challenges, but not all align with personal or preferred approaches to leading change for improvement. There is a noted gap in much of the research around leading improvement. Macklin and Zbar, in their book *Driving School Improvement,* have scrutinised many different and popular leadership frameworks from around the world and found that "almost all the frameworks examined fall short as far as ensuring effective leaders of school improvement is concerned. This is because they tend to focus entirely on the capacities individuals need to develop to become and remain leaders in their school, without reference to what leaders actually need to do to drive improvement in their schools" (2020, p. 23). Examples of clear capabilities and skills that are essential to be a successful, high-performing leader are found in the Australian Institute for Teaching and School Leadership Standards (AITSL 2017). AITSL have published research-based "Principal Standards" organised under three Leadership Requirements:

1. Vision and values
2. Knowledge and understanding
3. Personal qualities, social and interpersonal skills

And five Professional Practices:

1. Leading teaching and learning
2. Developing self and others
3. Leading improvement, innovation and change
4. Leading the management of the school
5. Engaging and working with the community.

Few leadership researchers would deny that the AITSL 2017 leadership standards are essential skills of a leader. These capabilities, when activated appropriately, will characterise a well-rounded leader who has the suitable attributes to lead a successful school or organisation. However, the missing link, as highlighted by Macklin and Zbar (2020), is that these standards, like many other leadership frameworks, identify the capacities but not an effective process by which to best activate the appropriate capability or resource to get the best improvement outcomes. Within all leadership opportunities I have encountered, I have built an understanding of what skills or capabilities I may require to ensure I have the best influence on the people I am leading. The conflicting view of having effective or developed capabilities is how do I implement them in a consistent, effective and balanced way?

Leadership learning link

The critical missing link between our leadership capabilities and the actions that are clearly communicated to leaders in school is what I refer to as the "leadership learning link". This is where the "how" of leading sustained improvement sits perfectly. As Macklin and Zbar argue, research consistently identifies very common attributes, skills, knowledge and strengths that together ensure successful leadership. I would argue that almost all school systems would have different varieties of clearly defined actions; for example, data-driven targets and goals, accountability assurance processes, and annual or longer-term improvement planning documentation. However, the essential ingredient for leading improvement at any level is how we lead people. Outstanding leadership capabilities or expert knowledge of actions have limited potential if we do not know how to take the teams we are leading along with us. The SKIM Model sits comfortably within the gap in our leadership development, providing an opportunity to harness our personal capabilities through leading our teams to achieve our actions.

Jim Knight (2011) asks a key question that I believe all leaders should ask themselves as they embark on any approach where they are attempting to lead change: "what do we desire as educational leaders?" In answering this open question, leaders can begin the process of identifying their destination for change and ultimately improvement. Just as important is planning the process of how you intend to lead your team to that destination and what capabilities you need to lean on or develop to ensure you are in the best position professionally to implement an effective improvement process.

I have had the privilege of leading several different organisations and have had a positive influence on many adults and students in my various leadership roles. I am fortunate to be in a position to continue to influence as an active leader of people. As leaders we can have an impact on hundreds if not thousands of lives both directly and indirectly. We are not leading for our own importance; we lead to get the best out of others, because we know we can have a positive influence and help others reach their potential.

Likewise, writing this book is to share a framework that I know can help others as it has helped me. The SKIM Model will create an environment that allows you to continue to develop your essential leadership capabilities, while providing you with the critical framework to apply your outstanding leadership skills to get the best outcomes for improvement. Leadership capabilities are intricate, and none of us will ever become an expert in every one of them. We have different skills that complement different situations. An effective leader can recognise their strengths and areas that might be a little shallow in skill acquisition. Identifying is the first step, followed by an intentional focus on finding opportunities to develop and apply those skills in your leadership process.

Much of the research on leadership and change suggests you need a high level of commitment from staff before you can embark on a successful change process, some suggesting up to 75% is needed before effective change can occur. However, the SKIM Model is moving the spotlight from investing energy in areas in which you will get little to no traction towards the small, subtle but important changes that will mean the "few" that engage will quickly become the "many". Right through the SKIM Model you will be leading improvement, one intentional step at a time. As Munby proposes, "ultimately, leadership is about making a positive difference, not just to organisations (although that is essential) but also to its people – and, in education, to the lives of children and young people" (2019, p. 273). What a privilege that responsibility is.

In leadership, the complexities are immense, and change is heavily impacted from a level of contextual understanding. I firmly believe that "leadership" as a model is not exclusive to an organisation or a role – for example, being a principal of a school or a CEO of a company. Tracey Ezard describes leadership in her book *Ferocious Warmth* as a process that is "full of contradictions. Without them, leadership would be a walk in the park. We could make decisions quickly and easily, as the answer would be straight forward" (2021, p. 41). Changing the narrative that leadership styles are exclusive to a particular organisation allows the core elements of strong, research-based leadership to be transferred between organisations. I firmly believe that the core framework or model for effective and high-level improvement leadership is in actuality simple and not overly complex. The complexity is built from the people and contexts in which you lead. Michael Fullan, in his book *Motion Leadership*, suggests that successful improvement and change leadership involves strategies that have "the appearance of simplicity whilst at the same time unleashing powerful and in many ways marvellously complex processes" (2010, p. 4).

Michael Fullan and Joanne Quinn, in their book *Coherence*, take this concept further, coining the term "simplexity". They describe the improvement process as identifying some small steps or factors to solve a difficult problem, "the simple part. And then make these factors gel under the reality of action with its pressures, politics, and personalities in the situation – this is the complex part" (2016, p. 127). There is no "silver bullet" in leadership; however, the SKIM Model will turn the unnecessarily complex into a process of simple, predictable yet highly empowering levels of improvement through intentional leadership. The SKIM Model is simple, easy to implement and is a routine or process that can be transferred to any leadership situation. As Fullan has indicated through his research, the complexity of implementation is building meaningful relationships and understanding your people.

What have I learnt from Alfred?

During my experiences as a senior leader, I have continuously evolved my understanding of what successful leadership looks and feels like, and based on research, I have built a model that I have tried and tested in many different and varied organisations. We have identified that people are complex, we lead staff in building their capacity to deliver new and innovative ways to achieve better outcomes, we lead the building of a collective student voice and understanding around agency as our students develop into young, positive, active citizens, and we lead families and communities, with the school being a micro-municipal environment that strongly reflects the values and expectations of the outside community. What a challenge! So how do you do that in an effective, efficient, positive and manageable way?

We must acknowledge that leaders are also humans who, even with the best intentions, make mistakes or errors in judgement. This is unavoidable; however, it is how we manage these errors or mistakes, learn, and acknowledge them with our teams that build a culture of trust. As Munby highlights, "good leadership is not about never having a bad day – we are human, after all. It is about getting up and starting all over again when you have a bad day because that is what leaders do!" (2019, p. 54). There is a poignant line in Christopher Nolan's Batman movie "The Dark Knight", released in 2008, where Alfred, Bruce Wayne's loyal butler, imparts some perfect "leadership" advice emphasising the importance of learning from failure and picking yourself back up when things have not gone the way you had expected.

Alfred: "Why do we fall, sir? So we can learn to pick ourselves up."

When I think about the most significant "pick ourselves up" leadership learning moments in my life, I focus on my parents and a particular moment that changed our lives and knocked us all to the ground. My mother and father were amazing leaders in their chosen professional fields. Dad was a chef who received many accolades, one of which was cooking for the royal family in a restaurant he worked at in England, well before I was born. Mum was a teacher, then principal. She had a passion for small rural schools, where she could lead school improvement while also having an ongoing direct connection to teaching in the classroom. Growing up for me felt normal; however, it might be viewed as a little bit unusual by others. Our family owned pubs: a bar for those who wanted a drink and restaurants for those who wanted a feed. From the age of two, I lived with my family on the third storey of the pub. Mum and Dad worked long hours, but I still remember having adequate family time. Their day would begin early with some kitchen prep. My sister and younger brother and I would wander down to the kitchen for brekkie before heading to school. Mum would teach during the day and then come home to run the restaurant front of house at night. Dad would bounce between kitchen and bar through the day, ensuring all staff went on their breaks while overseeing the running of the venue. Once meals were completed for the night, both Mum and Dad would return to the bar to close for the night. Mum would also fit some time in for her preparation for the next day back in the classroom.

Sunday was always a family day. The pub was shut, and the venue became a child's playground, with darts, pool tables, and plenty of places to play hide and seek. The business was highly successful, and although the work was significant for my parents, as a kid I loved growing up there. Not many young primary school-aged children would know what or who a "bar fly" was. This was a customer that spent an excessive amount of time in the bar, often socialising for long lengths of time, and like a fly would turn up and disappear with a level of regularity. Or there was the "bar moth" – like the bar fly but attracted to the establishment as soon as the lights were turned on.

Growing up in an environment such as this is something I attribute some of my leadership success to in later life. I was sheltered from a lot of the negativity or "drunkenness" that these types of establishments often witness. I learnt how to talk to people of all types from diverse backgrounds. I would listen to stories or watch magic tricks performed by the patrons. Some would bring their kids for my siblings and I to play with. One taught me how to play the trumpet; another was a sign-writer who gave me a painting lesson – these are only a few examples of the many different connections I was able to make. I often would win the raffle prize for the most money raised at my primary school. I had an effective plan: I got home from school, then completed a lap through the bar with my raffle sales pitch. A few hours later, I would come back and sell again. By then, many of the patrons had enjoyed a few hours of additional drinking. "Haven't I already bought one of these?" "Not that I can remember!"

All this success came crashing down for our family one night with an incident that took less than three minutes. A young man dropped into the pub late one night on his way to his mother's house to buy a six-pack of beers as take-aways. He wasn't a local and had just decided he needed some beer as he passed our venue. Unbeknown to my parents, this man had picked a considerable fight with a well-known bikie gang, and unbeknown to him, they had been following him that night, waiting for him to stop somewhere. That stop was our pub. The bikies were in and out in two minutes, and although the man survived the attack, they made their point very clear to him. Not a glass was broken nor a beer even spilt by anyone else that night. What followed was a series of events that ripped this successful business apart. The local media wrote on the front page that the incident was an organised brawl between rival bikie gangs, leading to the factually inaccurate reporting that my family's pub was a local "bikie hangout". Dad went from doing 300 meals on a Saturday night to only six. And those six were family friends who booked in to support my parents.

Our family sold the pub and had no option but to move into a caravan in the spud shed of my parents' best friends, the Boaks. I unfortunately had seen the aftermath the following morning when I came downstairs for brekkie, and I knew there was something big going on. But we were protected and buffered from things that would have further impact on our young worlds. The fall was substantial, however. In my later life I came to understand the considerable effort it took for Mum and Dad to pick themselves up. Mum became a principal around this time, leading others while experiencing the hardest time of our lives. Dad became a hospitality teacher at the local TAFE. To "pick themselves up", as Alfred explained to Bruce Wayne, Mum and Dad turned their energies to helping and leading others. This level of resilience and personal strength I have come to admire more as I reflect on what that time meant. In among all this upheaval, unpredictability and uncertainty, my siblings and I were guided on an unforeseen family adventure. What amazing parents, what amazing role models, what amazing leaders!

Please do not conclude from my example above that to be a good parent you must also be a good leader or vice versa. These are very different skills and demand very different approaches. What I have come to learn is that people in our lives have influence on us in many ways. People's influence is not always positive, and we must learn to navigate that and come out the other side stronger.

I can now see the level of calm and focus that my parents would have needed with what was going on in their world to not only lead but excel during this time in their professional and personal lives. They embraced change, they accepted challenge, they focused on building the capacity of others, getting on with their passions, rather than taking the "why me?" approach. They did all this while being great parents.

Cast the shadow you choose

To put it simply, leaders positively engage people, build their capacity to implement improvement initiatives, and measure the results in order to provide evidence of improvement. The challenge for any improvement agenda are the variables – not only the people that are being led, but the capacity and processes of the leader that is leading. As Munby (2019) argues, at times of change and uncertainty, leaders that are successful are those that do not see uncertainty as a deficit. They see it as an opportunity to add value or adapt to learn from and ensure future success. This idea is supported by Defour and Fullan: "if we know anything about change, it is that ordering people to change doesn't work" (2013, p. 33). For any leader, this would be an obvious statement. However, I would also be surprised if there is a leader who cannot remember a time when they felt they were being forced or pressured to engage in something they either did not agree with yet, weren't ready for, or did not feel they had the skills to implement. Thus, I would argue that this strategy, although it may be subtle, happens more regularly in organisations than the system is aware of. Defour and Fullan (2013) go on to describe effective change implementation: focusing on involving and engaging people in a process that binds people together, building with the majority while the sceptics become fewer and fewer. Knight supports the binding nature of the connection between learning and improvement with his statement "learning is infectious, energizing, and humanizing. Learning helps us live fuller, richer lives. When we are engaged in learning, our imagination, brains, and hearts all come alive" (2011, p. 45).

This book will provide you with a framework that will simplify your leadership process, allowing you to take control of the perfect improvement strategy, or as I describe it, the perfect "skimming stone" that will create multiple ripples with a simple, yet highly efficient model. Following this pattern of performance and strategic, intentional practice, you will be able to minimise sceptics while achieving positive implementation of leading change.

The SKIM framework will give you permission to "play the long game", to "move slow to move fast", while having a significant impact and maintaining the positive level of engagement and culture among the people you lead. "As a leader you cast a shadow. You shape that culture. For most heads (leaders) this is a privilege, and why they chose to be a head – the opportunity to make a difference on a large scale" (Munby, 2019, p. 34). The SKIM Model will support you to have the greatest influence on positive change in your organisation on a large scale by casting the right shadow over the environment and, most importantly, the people you are leading.

Take control of your skimming stone. The more you practise the art of skimming stones, the more positive ripples you will make.

Leadership reflection task

- ☐ What do you desire as an educational leader? List your short-term and long-term desires. Be specific.
- ☐ What are the specific capabilities you must lean on and what are the areas you need to work on and possibly intentionally lean on more and be more aware of?
- ☐ Can you think of a time you have "fallen" and needed to pick yourself up?
- ☐ What skills, values or capabilities did you need to lean on to pick yourself up?

CHAPTER 3

Introducing the SKIM Model

The SKIM Model is an improvement initiative framework broken into five main stages or "skims", each of which is focused on a different team (see Figure 1 overleaf). Each stage creates a ripple effect that drives the momentum of the next team that you will engage in the learning process of leading improvement and implementation. The pace, engagement and team selection of each ripple in the SKIM Model is determined by the previous team's modelling, peer leadership, and evidence of improvement. Throughout this book, I will walk you through the SKIM Model, providing comprehensive and real-life examples of successful leadership, including situations where I have made mistakes, reflected, and ensured that I developed into a better leader.

Figure 1: The SKIM Model overview

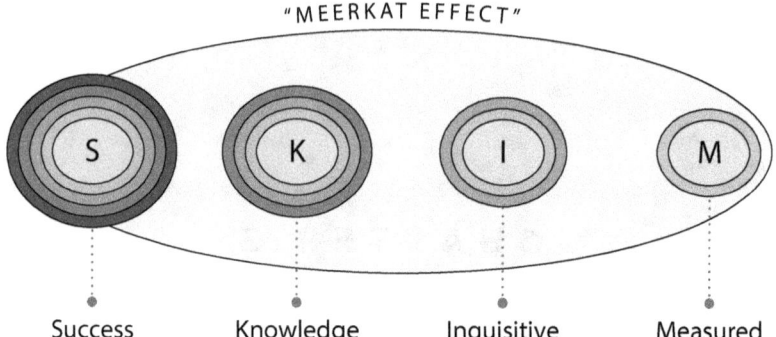

Success   Knowledge   Inquisitive   Measured

Success Team

The first lead team and the team all other staff are carefully watching.

Select the right team, not the easy team.

Use the 3Cs to support staff engagement.

This team's success will build the momentum for the Knowledge Team.

Knowledge Team

Actively watching the Success Team to build their understanding and capacity to engage.

Will not take a lot of energy to engage in the improvement strategy.

May naturally join the team, be selected or volunteer to engage in the improvement strategy.

Inquisitive Team

Are in need of strong evidence to build their interest in engaging.

Might have strong beliefs or values that are acting as barriers.

The Meerkat Effect will play a significant role in building their momentum.

Measured Team

Often portrayed unfairly as "the negative" staff.

They are an essential part of the improvement process.

This team force us to be a more informed leader.

They are only a small percentage.

You do not need to invest excess energy until it is their turn to engage.

Understand their beliefs and values before leading.

Meerkat Effect

Active positive exposure to all staff in an ongoing manner.

Like a Meerkat observing from the safety of their burrow, your SKIM teams will be looking for success and danger or risk before engaging.

All staff need to be celebrated and acknowledged.

The SKIM teams lead the Meerkat Effect through celebrating success and evidence of improvement.

Improvement momentum will be built or paused through implementation of the Meerkat Effect.

Persuasion/convincing staff to engage in improvement is **not** a Meerkat strategy.

The SKIM Model in context

Before we get started on discussing the model itself, it is important to put the SKIM Model into context. The SKIM Model is not a static model; it is dynamic. There is a continuum along which staff will move depending on many variables. Some of these variables might be but are not limited to:

1. The topic of the improvement (for example, English, mathematics, wellbeing) and where I believe my strengths lie.
2. How confident I am about the improvement agenda.
3. My relationship with the leader leading the improvement.
4. My values and beliefs about improvement or this particular agenda.
5. My previous experience of change or change trauma from perceived or similar improvement agendas.

Dinham (2011) argues that it takes time to change patterns of thought that support effective and lasting change. However, Covey (1989) suggests that the more you understand the people you are leading, the more you will appreciate them, the more reverent you will feel towards them. It is this reverence that will allow you to have a greater understanding of the drivers for staff to accept or challenge change and improvement agendas. I love innovation and feel motivated by a problem or challenge to solve. Most leaders would feel the same and reflect on their own excitement about leading different improvement agendas. However, there are still situations where I might be seen as one of the "hard to move" staff. The leader would need to work hard to convince me that my beliefs may be unintentionally, or at times intentionally, misguided or possibly that I need to have more flexible thinking. We all, even the greatest leaders, have the capacity to move along the scale from jumping on the improvement process right up to digging our heals in and not budging. It all links to our individual values and beliefs.

Grind my gears...

I am an avid coffee lover, which I am sure is no surprise for a long-time educator. My wife, who also loves coffee, and I have a coffee machine at home, which gets a good workout. Normally, we would both have a coffee in the morning during the work week. I might have a second on a weekend if the need arises, so over a year our coffee machine would punch out more than 700 coffees.

My wife, Jess, who during university worked at a café, can make a mean coffee; however, we have a "hard to move" scenario that plays out most mornings. It comes back to our own beliefs and what we value, which in this scenario is misaligned. Please note: I am not airing my "dirty laundry" but illustrating how simple beliefs when unacknowledged could turn into more than a trivial issue. Jess will often pour a coffee, then tap the head of the filter to get the bulk of the coffee grounds out, leaving the sediment in the filter. Jess's argument is that this has no bearing on the pour and can be cleaned once all the coffee has been made. "It is how we did it in the café." I have no café experience, but my embedded belief is that it will pour better with a clean filter. What I am getting at here is that there is no right or wrong; we simply have different beliefs. Jess's belief is not going to "persuade" me to change mine, and my belief will not "convince" Jess that I am right and cause her to start cleaning the filter.

This simple analogy, and I am sure we all have different versions of this in our personal and professional lives, is an example of how small, misaligned values or beliefs can turn into larger, more pronounced problems or conflict. If a leader came to me and simply said, "Steve, it is OK to leave the sediment in the bottom of the filter – it has no impact on your coffee", you might not see the innovative, change- and improvement-focused leader I am. Instead, you might get a rebuttal, one that is full of my facts, my experiences, and my beliefs, whether accurate or not. You would need to work hard to move me from this belief, because it negatively impacts me.

Imagine that I had a strong belief about the way I was teaching reading. Right or wrong, I have built this belief over years. A simple "this is now how we are going to do it" will not change this belief, and you will most likely receive a return of serve of what is often seen as negative, disrespectful or "blocker" behaviour. But this is simply a staff member telling you, sometimes not in the most appropriate or professional manner, that you have not proven to me that your improvement agenda is better than what I currently do, what I currently value and believe in. Prochaska et al. (1994) suggest that many people are simply unaware that they need to change. "Research on attitudinal change has long found that most of us change our behaviors somewhat before we get insight into new beliefs" (Fullan, 2010, p. 25). Yet leaders can often invest a lot of energy into changing a few staff members' beliefs with minimal success. We focus on the hard-to-move rather than the keener-to-move staff because we start an improvement process with an unintentional deficit approach. "Will Steve whine about his issue with coffee grounds in the filter this time? Why can't Steve just accept that this is not a problem for anyone else, so why should it be one for him?"

My perception is my reality

Now think of your staff, and as we move through the SKIM Model, reflect on their personalities and the belief systems that they value. Do not assume that "Steve" is going to be a challenge in leading this improvement process. If you already have that opinion before entering the SKIM Model, you are closing your mind to potential leading and learning opportunities. Instead, think like an open-minded leader: "What do I need to do to lead Steve to the improvement destination?" My mind, values or beliefs will not change by themselves; I will need to be led to a different belief, and that takes time. Research will continue to argue that adult learning cannot be addressed with the same principles as teaching our students. In his article "Andragogy, not pedagogy", Knowles (1968) argues that adults need five key elements for effective learning:

1. Self-concept – adults are self-directed learners.
2. Experience – an acknowledgement that adults have a range of experience, knowledge, and ideas.
3. Readiness – adults want to learn things that are relevant to real-life contexts.
4. Orientation – adults need learning that is problem-centred and practical.
5. Motivation – adults are intrinsically motivated by factors such as self-esteem, job satisfaction, personal growth or development.

Adults are complex beings who require acknowledgement of their individual beliefs, values and personal attributes. The worldly and community expectations or complexities are increasing, and as leaders we must slow the pace and allow our adult learners to engage at a pace they are comfortable with. When I started teaching, there was an unwritten rule – and maybe it was articulated to me by some of the more experienced teachers – "Leave your personal baggage at the front gate." As I have progressed through my teaching and leading career, and read research around mental health and wellbeing, I have come to realise that this idea of leaving your world at the gate is not realistic. Please do not get me wrong – we are professionals, and we have a level of expectation around our conduct, how we act, perform, communicate and respect our work environment – however, when I look at my staff sitting around a staff room table, I see a different view than the younger me.

I see:

- A teacher who is learning their craft as a graduate, is strong and resilient, but is feeling overwhelmed by the demands of their new profession.
- An aspiring leader, who has put their hand up for a responsibility and is feeling the pressure of performance and not wanting to let the principal or their teaching team down.
- A staff member who has recently disclosed mental health challenges and has started on medication to support their health and life balance.
- A staff member who is having relationship troubles and has requested leave to get personal guidance.
- A staff member who has a child in senior secondary school who is struggling with the workload and motivation.
- A staff member who is thriving and loving life as a professional. However, I am aware that they will say yes easily and if not managed could become overloaded.
- A staff member who has conflict with another member of staff, and it is becoming more apparent in the staff room.

I would be surprised if there is not a staffroom in any organisation that does not have similar, but different, versions of the above. As a leader, the challenge is then: How do you lead your team with empathy and understanding while still having high expectations? Along with the "naughty kid" stereotype, we have the "naughty staff" stereotypes. I am sure we have all been in a position where we have come across the "naughty kid", and before they have a chance to be naughty we already have the belief that they are, either because we have been told they are or because we have witnessed something that is now embedded in our beliefs. So what happens? This person then lives up to our perception because we are looking for and expecting that behaviour. The people we lead are no different. If we have an embedded belief about their "naughty staff" profile, we may lose sight of the great things they have to offer in our improvement processes. Wiliam (2019) suggests "if we create a culture where every teacher believes they need to improve, not because they are not good enough but because they can be even better, there is no limit to what we can achieve". Some staff members are at a cognitive spilling point before they have started the day (see Chapter 5, "Unload your cognitive load"). However, we know the implications of a clear, transparent framework that is process-driven and supports learning by reducing the pressure on short-term memory. The SKIM Model, once practised and embedded, can become a routine that sits in your long-term memory and creates space for new learning to grow and develop, provides time to differentiate and focus on the individual support your team needs, and allows you to be the leader they need you to be.

It's time to pick the right stone to make sure you become a skimming expert.

Leadership reflection task

- [ ] What does your staff room look like (experience, relationships, personal challenges, perceived conflict)?
- [ ] How do you differentiate your leadership approach based on the knowledge you have of the people you lead?
- [ ] Without naming names… Is there a naughty kid/staff belief that could influence how you lead or approach your teams or individuals? If so:
- [ ] How might you intentionally adjust this perception?

CHAPTER 4

Selecting the right skimming stone

The SKIM model (Figure 2) streamlines the improvement process from the beginning until the desired outcome or until we need to pivot to the next phase of improvement. I was once told by a mentor that improvement is a destination you never arrive at. The fact that you "never arrive" sounds a little depressing when you are working in the space of leading improvement. However, the underlying meaning of this view is that as they get closer to the original improvement destination, good leaders are already in the midst of moving the finish line further away to the next aspirational target.

Figure 2: The SKIM Model

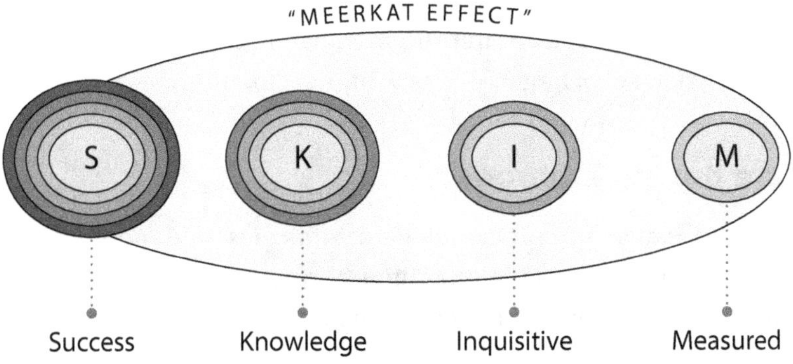

"MEERKAT EFFECT"

S — Success
K — Knowledge
I — Inquisitive
M — Measured

A good walk ruined (Mark Twain)

I like to think of improvement a little like my golf game. I love golf, but golf seems to dish up a lot of challenges and frustrations for me. Yet, I keep coming back for more. Golf would be such an easy game if I could hit the ball straight or at least close to where I want to. I would reach the green quicker, with less shots, my overall feeling of success would be much higher, and my overall efficacy would increase. However, in reality I tend to explore most of the grass and trees to the side of the fairways, all the way to the green. Do not get me wrong: I aim to hit the ball straight, but more often than not the ball has a mind of its own. Like a newborn giraffe, I stagger and zigzag all over the course.

Improvement is similar: if it were easy to head in a straight direct line to the required improvement destination, it would be much easier and more achievable, but that is not the reality. We will zigzag all over the improvement approach. Like golf, I will keep coming back to lead more improvement, even though it is challenging and messy and I must sometimes go searching for the ball. However, the feeling of success, celebrating the small wins, seeing the strategy working, observing the changes in the team you are leading – these things make it all worthwhile. That is why leaders keep pursuing improvement. Be prepared: there will be few hits that will result in the ball heading straight down the fairway. Again, like golf, the more you practise implementation of your improvement model, the better, more consistent, more predictable, and more efficient you will become at leading.

Like my golf game, improvement is a destination I am aspiring to arrive at but will never quite reach. If I could hit the ball consistently straight, my next steps in improvement would focus on how to master another skill such as bunker shots, putting, or having a greater control over the ball's distance. You never get to the peak of improvement without having another hill to climb with a new set of targets or a new improvement strategy.

We are not superheroes

With many leadership methodologies, strategies and approaches are available to support – or sometimes hinder – your work as a leader. Leaders need to be careful to ensure they are selecting the right process that aligns with their organisational goals, vision, resources and people. The SKIM Model is an adaptable framework that gives leaders the scaffold to overlay their organisational context within the model. You dictate the goals, the resources, the strategy and the context of your organisation, and the SKIM Model will support you by reducing your cognitive load (discussed in Chapter 5), providing the framework to move through the apparent challenges or turn the perceived complex into the actual "simplexity" in a consistent, predictable and measurable manner.

Leadership is about being authentic, genuine or as it is colloquially called, being human. We are not superheroes; we have strengths and weaknesses. The more we lean on our strengths, while being vulnerable or open to support and growth in our weaknesses, the more human we are perceived to be. This perception is incredibly important to those that you lead. We make mistakes as humans; we acknowledge these mistakes, work to rectify or mend the error, and use it as an opportunity to learn ourselves, while leading others to be open and honest about our individual areas of need.

It is important to acknowledge, however, that change and improvement are not always correlated with positive outcomes. Robinson (2018) discusses how change is to move from one state to another, but the new state may be better, worse or the same as the first. Improvement, on the other hand, suggests that you are influencing others in order to leave the situation in a better state than before. Robinson's conclusions about change and improvement are an important link when we are discussing the significance of the selection of the appropriate improvement strategies or focus areas in leading change for improvement.

The first stage of the SKIM Model, with its metaphor of skimming a stone, is the selection of the right stone. For those of you who have spent time on a riverbank trying to skim the perfect stone, you may have noticed how much time you have spent searching through the many different stones on the bank looking for the perfect one. In this process, you will drop more stones than you skim, picking up and dropping stone after stone until the right one catches your eye – the "perfect stone". We can compare this with the process for selecting the right improvement strategy for your organisation. You will need to be thorough and scrupulous when searching for the right strategy for your team, your improvement targets, your students, your staff, your leaders, or your community. You will need the courage to say "This is not the right strategy or project for us right now" more often than you will be saying "Yes, this is what we need next for improvement".

As a leader, I found this part of the process often the most challenging – the perceived or actual external pressures of new initiative after new initiative, as well as internal pressures of data analysis that might not be in line with your current area of focus or goals. However, saying respectfully to a staff member or a system leader "I love that idea, but it is not quite in line with our current focus – can we revisit it later?" takes a level of leadership strength that is needed to focus on the "less is best approach" that the SKIM Model will thrive on. Patrick Lencioni said it perfectly – "if everything is important, then nothing is" – or alternatively, if everything is high priority, then nothing is. Macklin and Zbar added that "schools need to have a very clear sense of where to start and focus their energies" (2020, p. 71). We have limited energy, and everyone's energy bank will vary based on multiple factors at any point of the day. A simple conversation or email could deplete your energy bank until you implement some personal strategies to get it back up. Therefore, we should not spend energy on things that will not have an impact or influence on the people of our communities.

I have personally made many errors through my career as a leader developing a plan or devoting time and energy to an initiative that has not succeeded or has resulted in minimal improvement based on the investment. It took my individual leadership development and reflective practice to understand why that might be. Most of the time, I would suggest it was me, my decisions, my pace, my misunderstanding, my lack of awareness of self and others, and importantly, my lack of emotional intelligence and relational trust of my staff. That is a hard cookie to swallow, but the reality is this is also how the adult learning process is expected to work.

Ratanjee argues: "Change initiatives often fail not midway through but at their very outset. An inaccurate, ambiguous, or misdirected definition of the change is primarily to blame" (2021, p. 2). Macklin and Zbar add that when leaders are focusing on what matters most, it brings "the associated challenge of being prepared to abandon those activities that effectively have less 'bang for buck' so the effort, resources, and time they involve can be directed to higher leverage strategies that will genuinely improve the school" (2020, p. 71). We must be aware of the improvement decision we are making and how this may impact the people we are leading.

How could I get this wrong?

It is always a good idea to ask yourself the reasons for perceived urgency in leading change quickly, bearing in mind that that quick change may lead to disengagement through a lack of genuine consultation. It may also create a process that lacks scrutiny and rigour around the purpose and vision of the decision to lead change. Many times, these difficulties take more time to resolve than slowing down the original consultation and involving the right staff or leaders from the beginning of the process would have done.

I often reflect on my decision to prioritise or to park an initiative or improvement strategy and ask myself a simple question that has very complex answers: "What would it look like if I get this wrong?" supported with the reflection question "What would I need to DO to get this wrong?" The purpose of these questions is to consider and plan for the challenges that I might face, the steps that might cause issues, and what I should do to avoid minimising the improvement impact. The answers vary according to the task or initiative and who I am leading, considering my understanding and relationship with them. The "who" are the team that will be impacted most if I get the process wrong. Now, that's motivation enough to get it right the first time.

Tracey Ezard, in her book *Ferocious Warmth*, describes leadership as a way of being, not doing. It is nebulous and elusive. It is as much to do with feeling and energy as thinking and planning (2021, p. 10). I cannot fault this idea considering leaders that are planning improvement or change. However, like the iceberg metaphor, the people I am leading often only see what the leaders are doing, so the meticulous understanding of "the doing" or the visible leadership is essential in the overall impact of leading improvement.

In my early senior leadership days, I was an energetic, enthusiastic, "head down, bum up" leader. Although I still have many of those qualities, I have learnt to regulate and lean on them when I need to. It's a little like when Peter Parker first worked out he was Spider Man: it took a while for him to learn how to control the web and use it for good not evil. My out-of-control web was simple: I loved and thrived off innovative change and improvement, but never considered for any length of time that many of my staff feared change. They did not like the unpredictability, the impact, or the feeling of needing to get back into the productive struggle of the learning pit, or in some cases they had "change trauma" from previous experiences.

The right stone with the wrong technique

I often reflect on one particular "skimming stone" (targeted improvement) selection, and I never got to find out if I had picked the right stone or not. I never got the opportunity to fling it at the water to see if it skimmed, because I assumed commitment, that my team were as passionate about this strategy as I was. I was leading change, but the jury was out as to how I was leading improvement. Wiliam (2003) explains that there is an assumption when we are considering professional adult learning with teachers based on the idea that teachers lack knowledge. That was my starting point, and wow, how did I get it so wrong?

Michelle was a very experienced teacher, a trained coach, and had an enormous amount of content and instruction knowledge. I had just started, as a young, fresh-faced, Energizer bunny leader. Immediately I was challenged by Michelle in a way that set the scene for a great deal of reflection and growth in my personal leadership approach. My curriculum knowledge was continuously under fire, and I was feeling the pressure from being questioned and doubted in front of my other staff. As a leadership team, we had been discussing a new literacy initiative, and I jumped at the chance to champion its trial. It was my big opportunity to not only prove my commitment and knowledge in leading initiatives in my new role, but also to set the tone for my leadership agenda. And that is where I went wrong: "*my* leadership agenda". I soon learnt that it never was and never should have been my agenda.

I assumed that my staff (particularly Michelle) were starting with a lack of knowledge, but in reality I was the one with a lack of knowledge, and this was highlighted at the very first meeting. Michelle had gotten wind of the trial, and before I could open the meeting, she stood up at the front and began to rattle off the research that debunked the initiative, followed by a list of reasons why this initiative was not appropriate and which initiative would support better improvement. I was stunned, unprepared and quite defensive. I had not considered any of these arguments as possibilities, while having false confidence in my agenda.

In the book *Think Like a Monk*, Shetty (2020) explains that when we are humble, we are open to learning because we understand how much we do not know. He argues that the biggest obstacle to learning is being a know-it-all. This false confidence is rooted in the ego. My ego was driving my leadership and how I was selecting my skimming stones. I was unable to be honest, humble, or most importantly, vulnerable, failing to acknowledge what I did not know while not being open to learning from others who had more knowledge than I did.

If I were in this unlikely position again, we would never have got to this stage, for many reasons, the most important of which is that, on reflection, I was not leading. I was not selecting the skimming stone with my team in mind or the context in which I was leading. I had not considered the already strained relationship I had with Michelle and how I was going to lead her by acknowledging and harnessing her strengths. I had not reflected on "How could I get this wrong? What would that look like?" More importantly, Michelle was right: I had not considered alternative views. As Wehmeyer and Zhao (2020) explain, when schools are structured around control, standardisation and compliance, among the first things to be lost are trusting, meaningful relationships. I would argue in this case that it was not the school's structure that got in the way and further damaged an already complex relationship; it was my approach, my decisions, and my inexperience.

Jim Knight sums up my experience, explaining that "when we take our assumptions for certainties, it leads to many conflicts and failures", going on to argue that "when we have faith in others, we let go of the notion that we need to control them, tell them what to do, or hold them accountable. We see people as autonomous individuals deserving of our respect" (2011, p. 40). So, the big question is, how do I pick the right skimming stone? The simple answer is: carefully. "The default approach to change that most schools adopt is to accumulate new strategies, add them to those they are seeking to implement and never abandon anything" (Macklin & Zbar, 2020, p. 10).

The careful selection of your skimming stone is the first and most crucial decision to make to drive your improvement agenda so as not to accumulate unnecessary improvement agenda items. Remember that you will drop more stones than you skim, and you must accept that one of your greatest challenges in this space is having the confidence to say, politely and respectfully, "*No*, that is not for us right now."

Lead your leaders

In introducing the skimming stones metaphor, I discussed the process of walking the bank with my kids, picking up and dropping stones. I want to highlight the pride and engagement I had when my kids showed interest; I immediately became someone that could support their development in this simple, yet complex skill. Now, reflect on what we are trying to achieve, which is improvement, and think of my kids as my leadership team. You are building your leaders' capacity to select the appropriate skimming stones in collaboration with you, standing beside you. Imagine how much this will enhance your success and improvement opportunities.

Defour and Fullan (2013) discuss how for sustained improvement we are required to develop many leaders at all levels who learn through their colleagues. More gets done because you have more people leading the work and following the same agenda. You will end up with a "pipeline of leaders feeding forward to continue and deepen the direction of continuous improvement" (p. 64). This takes time and intentional strategic planning. Many teachers do not see themselves as leaders. I argue that every teacher is a leader of learning, and if you can align the passion and engagement they have as educators into an improvement process, the empowerment you will give staff will be significant. The SKIM Model is a framework that will scaffold leadership to lead leaders to lead. With the support of the SKIM Model, you will be leading staff who will in turn be leading the improvement strategy in their learning spaces and among their colleagues without the need to label themselves "leaders". This will begin the ripple effect of improvement through your organisation.

The most common feedback I have received in schools when I speak to staff about implementation or management and support of change is "I need more time". Unfortunately, I must break it to staff, I am not planning to extend our days, and the time we currently have is locked in. I am being a little facetious, as this is a legitimate piece of feedback; however, as we build the capacity of others to engage and see the importance of the area of improvement, the *value* of the improvement agenda often starts to take the focus over *time*. We reassess our priorities, and something new moves to the top of our list. Leaders must understand the burden that we place on staff and ensure that staff are not given more than they are capable of handling, emphasising the significance of a differentiated approach to adult learning.

It should be no surprise to leaders that not all staff have the same capacity, knowledge, experience, or strength of resilience. As Knight explains, "teachers are not workers on assembly lines, and they are not working with inanimate objects. Teachers are living, breathing, complicated professionals, and they work with living, breathing, complicated young human beings. To bring about improvement we want to see, we need to recognise – in fact honor – the complexity of providing support within professional relationships" (2011, p. 20).

The SKIM Model primarily is about understanding the relationships you have with your people. Michelle and I had a fractured relationship; however, if Michelle were in the school I am leading today, my approach and engagement with her would be a polar opposite to my ego-driven approach many years ago. I would recognise and acknowledge Michelle's strengths and harness them to support the process of change for improvement rather than oppose it based on conflict. Michelle had strengths that I was too proud to acknowledge. I felt they might undermine my leadership status. In hindsight, Michelle could have been my biggest improvement ally.

I have developed the SKIM Model over several years and experiences. As with any learning process, most of my learnings have been from when I "stuffed up" or things didn't go to plan. On reflection, the errors gave me clarity around the leader I need to be to drive improvement – more importantly, the leader my staff need me to be to support them to continue to improve. As I moved from one school to the next, I learnt that the SKIM Model is a process that doesn't change in leading improvement: there are some key elements I need to invest time in and focus on; there are spaces I should devote my energies to and others I should not. Do not underestimate the knowledge required to implement this model or any other improvement model successfully. Every school I have led has needed a different version of me; I have had to lean on different skills and knowledge to lead improvement. The SKIM Model shaped the consistent and predictable framework for me to be adaptable enough to be the leader that the school needed me to be.

Defour and Fullan (2013) highlight a simple technique for leading improvement:

- To get anywhere you must do something.
- In doing something you have to focus on skills.
- Acquisition of skills requires clarity.
- Clarity results in ownership.
- Working together with others generates shared ownership.
- The deepest and most profound learning occurs through doing by taking action, seeing what works and what does not and trying again.

As a concept, leadership is a series of processes combined with a balance of values and moral imperative, and this also applies to the SKIM Model. However, as all leaders know, it is much more complex, and the main complexity comes from the people within the context you are leading. The SKIM Model, like any of the many models within the diversity of leadership research, will not take the action for you, nor will it make the decision on what is the right skimming stone for your improvement agenda. You will, as all leaders must do, make mistakes, reflect, learn from them, adjust and go again. The benefit of adopting the SKIM Model as your preferred leading improvement framework will be your opportunity to adjust or pivot leadership direction, maintain relational trust, minimise the impact of change fatigue, reduce your cognitive load as a leader, and lead your team with intentional clarity and direction.

Pick your skimming stone carefully, understand your organisation's values, direction and unique context. Most importantly, understand your people, as they will be your biggest allies walking alongside you on the riverbank.

Leadership reflection task

- ☐ Draw enough columns on a page to have each of your organisation's key goals/targets as the heading at the top of each column.
- ☐ Under each goal/target, list all the strategies or initiatives that you are leading to ensure achievement of that particular goal or target.
- ☐ Prioritise the strategies or initiatives, putting the one you believe will have the greatest influence on improvement at the top, with the one of least influence at the bottom.

Review your list:

- ☐ Do you have capacity for all the strategies or initiatives to be implemented effectively?
- ☐ Are you or your staff spread too thin with too many improvement strategies?
- ☐ Could you do less and do it better?
- ☐ Are there things that need to be parked now, things that need to be elevated and invested in more, or things that need to be stopped?

What is your reflection on the skimming stones you have selected for improvement?

CHAPTER 5

Unload your cognitive load

If you could unload your cognitive load by implementing a simple model, would you?

The cognitive load theory was formulated by Emeritus Professor John Sweller in the 1980s and is a framework that uses our knowledge of evolutionary psychology and human cognitive architecture as a base for instructional design (Sweller et al., 2011). It has been supported by much empirical research for decades. Before we enter the world of models and frameworks, I am going to address an important question that you might have: "Do I need a leadership model?" Firstly, great question: the answer I believe depends on your own values and leadership philosophy. However, the cognitive load theory suggests that having a framework in which you have clarity and a clear process to guide your decisions will in fact unload your cognitive load, giving you more short-term memory to focus on new learning, relationships and problem solving.

Sweller et al. argue that "in the absence of an appropriate framework to suggest instructional techniques, we are likely to have difficulty explaining why instructional procedures do or do not work. Lacking knowledge of human cognition, we would be left with no overarching structure linking disparate instructional processes and guiding procedures" (2011, p. v). Frameworks support both process and consistency, identifying where things may have gone wrong, while also alleviating your short-term memory, placing the process into the long-term memory to retrieve as you need it rather than "thinking on your feet" about "what do I need to do next?"

The cogs of education

One of the core principles of the cognitive load theory is that the working memory is limited in its capacity to process information. When humans are presented with too much information, it overloads our working memory. My wife would argue that she sees this regularly with me. I get home from work – let's say it has been a rough day in the office and I have had to deal with some higher-level issues or incidents. On top of this, I may have had a parent call that I had to follow up and a staff member that required support with a student. I get home, and my wife gives me two very simple instructions. I nod, and then go and do something completely irrelevant to what was asked of me. She gets frustrated, I don't understand why, and so on and so on. The reality is: my cognitive load is overflowing, and I am finding it difficult to process any additional information in my short-term memory, as small as it might be. It is overflowing, and anything new has no space to settle in.

I see this from my staff from time to time, when they have had a rough day and I get a call to come and "support" them. Often I get there to offer my services to find that what they are actually asking is "Please sort this out for me. I don't have the space in my working memory to regulate and implement a new or different process or approach. I need time and space to recalibrate" – or something of that nature, not with words, but through their disposition. Only recently I got this very call. I read the situation wrong and handled it in a way that I thought was appropriate by explaining a recently implemented process that should be followed in this situation to minimise such challenges. It was when the teacher started blankly glaring at me that I realised he did not need advice; he needed me to take a little of his cognitive load off him to reduce the impact. This also highlights for me as a leader that the process had not been locked in this staff member's long-term memory. He was still working in his short-term memory and trying to think about the process and how to implement it, rather than the process being automatic, giving him the space to focus on his other skills to minimise the challenges. However, there may have been several things that had occurred that had filled this staff member's short-term memory, leaving him unable to access the appropriate process due to the flexible space having been filled.

The New South Wales Department of Education conducted a literature review in 2017 on the impact of the cognitive load on educators. One of their key findings was that the more complex or unfamiliar the learning is, the higher the cognitive load on our working memory. The easier or more familiar the learning is, the quicker our brains can process this and be ready for the next level of learning. Overleaf is an overview from the research that outlines how information is collected, processed and stored in our brains and importantly how the brain learns.

In our education environments, we have structures and frameworks that support predictable instructional techniques and support our staff to minimise their cognitive load. For example, few schools would not have a version of an instructional model. This is the perfect example of a framework that aims to reduce our staff's cognitive load. This may not have been the intention when you led the development or reviewed the consistency of these models; however, reducing a teacher's cognitive load is exactly what these instructional models are doing. Goodwin (2018) suggests that an instructional model provides the mechanism for teachers to support students in cementing new knowledge into their long-term memories while avoiding any cognitive overload. Not only does an instructional model support students' overload, but it also supports our educators. Macklin and Zbar go on to propose that "developing and implementing a whole school instructional model can provide the key means of improving planning and thereby building teacher capacity and driving better teaching through the school" (2020, p. 118). The design of the instructional model allows teachers to have a consistent and predictable routine such that, as the teachers gain confidence in each of the smaller elements of the model, they become more automatic, and less working or short-term memory is needed to think about the steps required. Instructional models are designed to optimise teacher impact by breaking a lesson into smaller parts, steps or stages, thus supporting the teacher to develop a level of automaticity. Please note, this automaticity is about process and structure, so that the remaining working memory space can focus on the students' needs, the differentiation, the engagement processes – the things that will have the greatest impact on your students.

Figure 3: How the brain processes new information and the impact on cognitive load (NSW Department of Education, 2017)

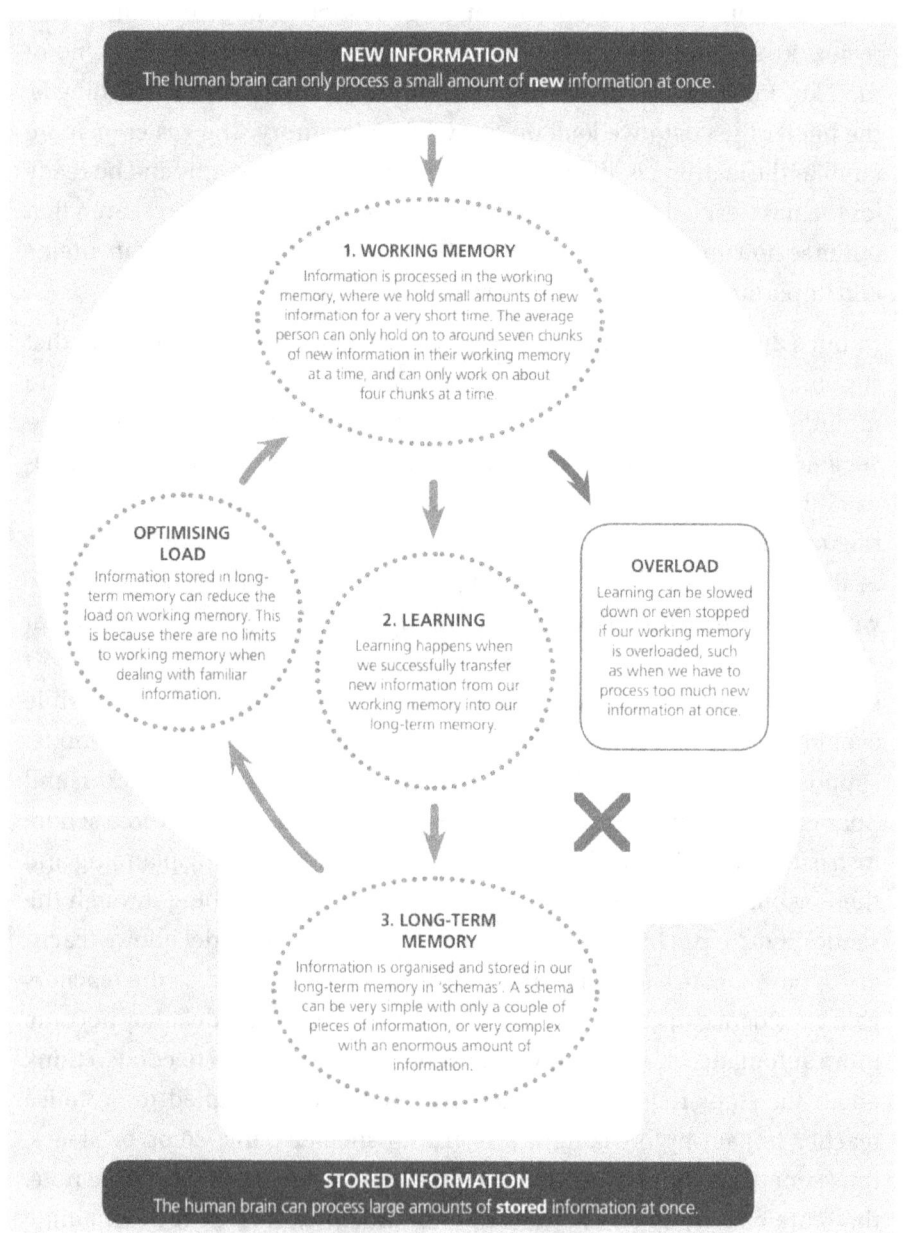

What is your model?

When I have asked leaders and colleagues "What is your leadership model?" I have often received a list of values in response, such as, but not limited to:

- Honest
- Trustworthy
- Fair
- Respectful

or a list of skills such as, but not limited to:

- Building relational trust
- Collaboration
- Distributive leadership
- Being approachable.

None of these are negative by any means and are essential capabilities and skills for good leadership. However, when a teacher enters their classroom with a new learning task, new student groupings, needing to differentiate, anticipating new directions or questioning, and thinking about how they will be providing the instructions, they require a strong understanding of their teaching and learning model so that they can manoeuvre or pivot at appropriate times and in a responsive manner for their students' needs. Imagine entering a leadership improvement strategy with a model that helps you lead change or improvement with a level of automaticity. Assume you are driving an improvement agenda in reading. You enter the staff room, and you have already identified the group of staff who will be your "champions" and lead the work (the "Success Team" – see Chapter 6). You have prepared for some of the push-back, and you are OK with that. You understand that your focus will not be attempting to engage every staff member today – that will take time and intentional leadership and strategy. You can now focus on leading the people, with their individual needs and differentiated adult learning, and importantly enjoying the improvement process.

Leading a school community through the worldwide pandemic was the first time I came across the cognitive load theory. I listened to a presentation by Kristen Douglas, the National Manager for Headspace, an Australian youth mental health foundation. Kristen was speaking to an online "room" full of principals. She put a graphic of a battery (Figure 4), on the screen and explained, pre-pandemic, how educators would work for a term reducing our personal energy battery or filling our cognitive load bucket. We would get to the holidays, and this would generally be enough time to recharge the battery and offload some of our cognitive load before returning to the work environment to go again. However, during the pandemic, our batteries drained, and we did not get any opportunity to recharge. We were leading our communities over the holidays, through the weekends, and after school hours. I felt this; I lived this. I had lost my routine, predictability and consistency, and I felt my cognitive load spilling over. I had lost control of my own systems and processes without notice. My students, staff and families were heavily relying on me, and I was feeling the pressure. It was at this point that I had to decide what was important and what was not for my community and myself as a leader.

My first step was to simplify and minimise our improvement agenda. I started to build new processes that were transferable and adaptable, like the SKIM Model, and turn the "less is more" approach from words to actions.

Figure 4: Illustration of battery, showing energy levels and overload if we don't have time to recharge (Kirsten Douglas, National Manager, Headspace, Australia)

Defour and Fullan, in their book *Cultures Built to Last*, highlight how "the constant crush of piling new disconnected, uncoordinated, fragmented change initiatives onto existing programs is more likely to result in educator confusion, exhaustion, and cynicism than improve student achievement" (2013, p. 29). As a young leader, I adopted an unintentional "lead as

I go" strategy. I knew the improvement agenda and had clarity on the improvement destination; however, my strategy was often unprepared or involved thinking on my feet. I called it "flexible" or "adaptable", but in reality, I made decisions as issues or problems arose, which meant I often had to double back and try again, and my cognitive load was constantly overflowing with new thinking or process development. I was being reactive rather than proactive. Staff would have felt confused and a level of cynicism when their leader was using flexibility as a strategy, though really it was an excuse for being unprepared.

Flexibility and adaptability, when implemented well, support good leadership practice. However, people are complex, and if leaders are not in a confident space to understand how we are going to lead our people, we run the risk of using our skills as excuses rather than as opportunities. Munro and Campbell explain how "the assertion that the work of educators is human intensive and complex rather than merely complicated is well established. This is supported by research and theory from non-educational organisational contexts" (2022, p. 28). There is no argument that leading people is complex. My question, then, is: "If you can minimise the complexity by adopting a framework that reduces your leadership cognitive load while giving you the guidance to lead quality improvement strategies, why wouldn't you?"

Fullan encourages leaders to employ strategies that are "going to have the appearance of simplicity while at the same time unleashing powerful and, in many ways, marvellously complex processes" (2010, p. 4). Fullan goes on to suggest that there is "too much overload and baggage on the current change journey" (p. 16). You can combine both of Fullan's learnings of leadership, adding in a simple framework that supports the outstanding growth and capacity building of our staff, while also minimising the "overload" of yourself as a leader. The NSW Department of Education (2017) research found that a key way to overcome the limitations of working memory is to ensure there are clear schema constructions. The SKIM Model provides both process and schema constructions with automation in an easy, effective and efficient manner.

In adopting a model such as the SKIM Model, you are opening space in your working memory for the people you lead rather than filling it with the "how" you are going to lead. By applying the cognitive load theory, and using a consistent framework like the SKIM Model, you will be able to create deeper, effective learning experiences that promote a depth of understanding and long-term memory retention.

Leadership reflection task

Reflecting on your task in Chapter 4 (listing all the improvement initiatives you are currently leading in your organisation):

- ☐ How many of these tasks are new learning for your staff?
- ☐ How many are building on existing skills?
- ☐ Can you reduce the new learning and increase the capacity building of existing skills to balance out the cognitive load of your adult learners?

PART 2
The SKIM Model

CHAPTER 6

Success

Figure 5: The SKIM Model: Success

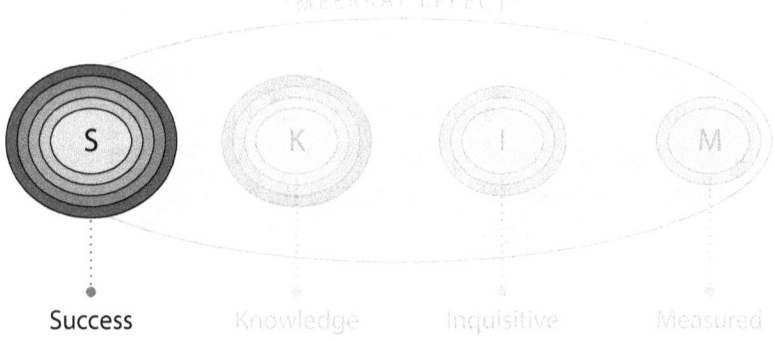

The definition of success is subjective and can vary from person to person. However, in general, it is the achievement of one's goals, objectives or desires that are significant or fulfilling. As with the definition, the measurement of success can differ from person to person, subject to subject, goal to goal. Ultimately, success is deeply personal and an individualised concept that can be interpreted differently by different individuals, depending on their values, aspirations, and circumstances. As a leader, you must articulate and provide clarity as to what "success" looks like during the implementation of an initiative or improvement agenda.

One fundamental question that you will need to address as a leader of improvement is: "How will we measure success?" As Defour and Fullan (2013) argue in their book *Cultures Built to Last,* hope may be a virtue, but it is not a strategy. They go on to suggest that one of the fundamental roles of a leader is to ensure that you create conditions that will allow the people you are leading to be successful in improvement. The SKIM Model will provide the framework for you to lead successful implementation of improvement; however, the first "skim", the carefully selected improvement agenda, the moment that the stone hits the water for the first time, is ultimately going to open the door to positive engagement in the improvement plan or guarantee your stone will sink to the bottom of the river with a splash rather than leaping off the water surface.

Remember, it is the responsibility of the leader to lead people to improvement, to ensure that the right structures and enablers are available and there is clarity in the direction and purpose. Smith (2005) states that change readiness is not automatic and cannot be assumed. I have walked into many staff meetings, over the years, inadvertently making assumptions that have backfired. Sometimes it is something as simple as discussing the procedures for editing family communication. In a quick conversation with my leadership team, we discussed a small editing process change. Instead of one other staff member reading the correspondence, I requested that each staff member share it with three other staff members to support a varied perspective when working through the editing process.

My approach was simple, a small adjustment or change in process to create a more thorough editing method. My assumption was that my staff would see what my leadership team and I did; however, they did not, and the discussion fell flat. Because of my assumption, I did not lead with clarity or transparency; in reality I did not lead – I assumed compliance. This seems like a minor example, but I have seen it on a larger scale. In a system leadership role, I have found that unwarranted assumptions are not uncommon. It may be a new initiative, with generally great research backing the project, and often there is a good level of support from the central office team. The initiative facilitators walk into a room full of senior leaders to present their project and simply say (to be a little satirical): "Here is our initiative. There is a lot of research to support it. You can read that in your own time, but because you are senior leaders, you get it. You will take this on. I am excited. I am sure you are as well. Thanks." Like our staff, leaders need to be led in order to lead others; we cannot assume that because I am wearing a "Principal" badge, I will simply comply, understand and be able to run with the new initiative without a good level of leadership leading me and my understanding.

Sharratt suggests that "our entire education system and school improvement work is predicated on a deep belief that teachers can, will, and must teach high standards and that all students can and will learn" (2019, p. 49). A fundamental to ensuring and setting high standards in our educational environment is to have a leadership framework that guides our staff to be educational leaders, where our teachers get excited about the potential they hold in their own development and there is a culture of purpose, where we are celebrating our colleagues' successes and striving to always be a little better than we were yesterday. Barth (2006) argues that without purposeful culture, improvement will not occur in any facet of the organisation. The SKIM Model still requires strong leadership qualities and capabilities that enhance your organisation's culture. By employing the SKIM Model in your practice, you will alleviate the need to overthink the intentional leadership strategies, because they will become routine, and instead you will be able to put more attention and energy into the people you lead, the relationships and the culture you are creating.

Let's get into success

The first step in a thriving SKIM Model is to ensure the "Success Team" of staff have the clarity and viable capacity to support and eventually lead the improvement focus. Schwartz (2004), in the book *The Paradox of Choice*, claims that creating structures that provide a direct line of sight and focus for human experience, while respecting the autonomy of each individual, will result in productivity, motivation and greater commitment to the identified focus area. However, we cannot confuse the Success Team as the easy group to lead. In Rogers' (1962) "diffusion of innovation" theory (discussed in Chapter 13), Rogers identifies the first 16% of staff as "innovators" (2.5%) and "early adopters" (13.5%). I am not going to challenge the numerous peer reviews and wide use of Rogers' research. What I will highlight is that the SKIM Model will direct your perspective on firstly how you decide who will lead your improvement focus, while also identifying which staff will have the capacity to achieve the greatest amount of success in the shortest amount of time.

In the numerous staff rooms I have been a member of, I can identify how my staff commonly responded to a newly introduced improvement agenda – excited, challenged and anywhere in between. However, if I considered this the standard response (negative or positive) for every improvement agenda that was introduced, without the possibility that I could change my leadership approach and thus possibly have an impact on their response, I would be leading with a fixed mindset, again getting caught by my assumptions. Munby suggests identifying the bright spots in our organisation and building on them, focusing relentlessly on developing capacity to improve teaching and learning (2019, p. 135). When I am considering my lead team (Success Team) in the SKIM Model, I know I can always rely on my "innovators" and "early adopters" to actively engage in the initiative being considered – my "easy" option to support the improvement agenda. We can argue this is because, irrespective of the initiative, they have a high level of relational trust in me as a leader and know my intention is nothing less than genuine. However, are these staff the *right* Success Team or the *easy* Success Team?

Dinham (2011) discusses how school leaders play a significant role in creating the environment for teachers to be able to teach to a high level and meet expectations. To effectively lead improvement with high expectations, we must recognise and acknowledge a genuine understanding of those that we lead. Intentionally identifying who, why and where to start will make sure your Success Team is the first "skim" of many, opening the opportunity for leadership momentum. Dinham goes on to state that great leaders know that "it is impossible to gain unanimous support, approval, and commitment from staff. Rather than try to move all staff simultaneously, they focus on those that are talented and committed and provide them with support (encouragement, time resource, professional development)" (2011, p. 56). This is not suggesting we ignore our slower to adopt staff or staff who challenge us (we will discuss this in later chapters). They will be provided with the appropriate support as we move through the rest of the SKIM Model. However, we first need the Success Team to lead the way and ultimately be successful.

The question is, then, how do I select the Success Team? When I have been considering my Success Team initially, I need to know and invest in my staff, their individual development, interests, strengths, and knowledge. There are three key areas I focus my attention on – the 3Cs – Context, Capacity, Culture:

1. **Context** – what is the focus area of the improvement and who among our staff have an interest, skill or knowledge in this area?
2. **Capacity** – who among our staff have the capacity to be the lead team – considering other commitments, responsibilities and individuals' wellbeing (cognitive load)?
3. **Culture** – what is the history of the focus area? Is there change fatigue or change trauma from previous experience? Are there embedded beliefs or values that could impact the improvement area of focus?

The 3Cs are quite open-ended, and every one of your staff will have areas within this that are strengths and areas that need some further attention or support at any one time. This assessment is intended to open your thinking about the opportunities within your staff to lead and build your team's capacity and confidence to have a positive influence on others. In reflection on myself as an inexperienced senior leader, my default when deciding on where to start implementation with my staff – particularly if I was feeling cognitively overloaded, under pressure, or feeling perceived urgency – was to focus on my easy options. The staff who would always be compliant would follow my instructions with few questions. This gave me the feeling of success, but the reality was I was getting traction in a space where I was most likely going to get it anyway, whatever initiative I selected and led. The staff who really needed the strong leadership, I thought… I will get to them later – a stalling tactic. The other consequence of frequently selecting the "easy" option in staff leadership is that these staff will eventually be cognitively overloaded as well. They will continue to be compliant, continue to take on your lead roles in learning, and you will eventually lose your most engaged staff.

Figure 6 provides prompt questions to consider when selecting your Success Team. Using these will provide an openness to your discussion, allowing you to focus on individuals who have capacity to influence others in a positive way. You will lead the right team. Throughout the additional ripples in the

SKIM Model (Knowledge, Inquisitive, Measured), you will see versions of these prompt questions to consider in leading the remainder of your staff in a strategic way, but none are more important for success than the first skim, the Success Team.

Figure 6: The 3Cs prompt questions

Context	Capacity	Culture
Prompt questions for selected area of improvement		
Which staff members have knowledge? Which staff members have interest? Which staff members have skills or training?	Which staff have reasonable time to be on a lead team? What responsibilities/commitments do staff members already have in other improvement areas? What is the staff member's current cognitive load? (professional and personal)	What are the beliefs and values this staff member holds? Does the staff member believe there is a need for improvement? How does the staff member respond to leading adult learning?

These prompt questions will not generate answers; the aim is that they will create curiosity, which will lead to making informed decisions about who, how and why you will be leading your Success Team. Munby (2019) states that, as a leader, you must become the strongest voice. He continues to propose that it is our job as leaders to support our staff to see what can be achieved and then to pursue it. This sounds amazingly easy; however, we know that leading people in a collective direction, with a strong purpose and vision for improvement, has many layers of complexity. Within the SKIM Model, you have permission to focus your attention where you will get the greatest amount of traction, while enjoying and celebrating the success of your whole staff. Great leaders focus on the successes of their team. They measure their success by that of those they lead. They celebrate with their team and learn alongside them. This celebration starts with the Success Team.

What does it look like if I get this wrong?

I mentioned in Chapter 4 that one of my self-reflection strategies is to consider, "What would it look like if I get this wrong?" Like much of the best learning, we need to reflect on how or why things did not work the way we had planned, so that we can adjust our processes for future strategies and not make the same error again. My school at the time was provided with the opportunity to implement a highly researched writing initiative that would be supported with professional learning and consultants to build the capacity of identified curriculum leaders, to then lead whole-school writing improvement. The research was strong, and my entire staff were ready for a refreshed focus on writing improvement. My leadership team was excited and felt confident about the initiative's goals. We had engaged in a few months of learning and team discussions and created a comprehensive implementation plan. The time came to start to introduce and model some of the new learning as a trial in our learning environments, to get feedback from the teachers and students, and to start to build a picture of what this looked like in our context.

Our leadership team selected our Success Team. We had robust discussions about who were the right members and who might be part of our second or Knowledge Team. We did not focus purely on the "easy" options, which, as we have discussed, are the staff that we know will get excited and straightaway pick up and run with the initiative. We had a clear understanding of the staff that would have a positive influence on others to support building the momentum. Using the SKIM Model, and what I thought was a thorough consideration of the 3Cs, the modelling began in the learning spaces. After only a couple of sessions, my literacy leaders made an appointment to see me. We sat down, and their opening statement was a collective, "We have selected the wrong staff member." They followed up by listing the staff member's push-back behaviours, their questioning of the research, and their lack of commitment to the initiative. The staff member, Ashley, had spent the first couple of sessions trying to find holes in the trial.

May I quickly add: although this behaviour is challenging and can create perceived conflict, such uncooperative behaviour is a fundamental leadership weapon for harnessing and developing your capacity as a high-level leader of improvement. Controversial, I know... we will touch on this in a later chapter.

I and my literacy leaders started to analyse how or why this wasn't as effective as we had planned. Using the 3Cs framework, we reviewed our decision.

1. Context

Ashley had a genuine love of teaching writing. She was initially very excited about the opportunity to build on her current knowledge and improve her writing teaching and learning. In our initial discussions she had identified her commitment to writing and the love of writing she wanted to inspire her students to have. Ashley had also done many different writing professional development sessions over her career and expressed she was open to learning new strategies.

2. Capacity

Ashley was currently not engaged with other specific instructional coaching. She did not have any heavy professional learning commitments and was open to learning opportunities. She had taken on a key role in supporting the planning for writing with her teaching team, so we identified that there would be a natural influence she would be able to have on her professional learning community (PLC) to support the next stages of the SKIM Model's momentum.

3. Culture

We had identified that Ashley already had a love of teaching writing. She was actively involved in our adult learning schedule and willing to contribute to staff discussions. She had previously been involved in coaching and peer observation, receiving feedback and using that to improve her practice.

Parallel to this, we had also identified that Ashley was not someone whom we would consider an "innovator" or "early adopter" (Rogers, 1962). However, she was someone who would have an influence on other staff members, so it was crucial that we were intentional in our approach to ensure the influence was positive and not negative. We thought we had the perfect Success Team candidate to kick off our SKIM Model.

So, what went wrong and what did we learn?

We failed to consider one key component of Ashley's values and beliefs and how our strategy of implementation might send the wrong message about our improvement agenda.

What are the beliefs and values this staff member holds about teaching writing?

What we neglected to consider was our approach to this staff member was too confronting. We had considered that the teacher valued and believed in their love of writing and teaching writing; however, this embedded belief also was the barrier we hadn't considered. As my literacy leaders stood in front of the class, excitedly and enthusiastically modelling a change in our writing teaching and learning processes, Ashley was standing back feeling that her love of writing and her teaching method were being threatened. Although this was a trial and no immediate change was expected, Ashley wasn't feeling the excitement; she was hearing a different conversation. We were unintentionally saying to Ashley through our actions: "The way you teach writing is not good enough – here is a better way." And as you would expect, the feedback reflected this. Ashley picked holes through the entire session and defended her method and processes with a determined, immovable passion. It was a light bulb moment for my team and me. We had to backtrack and refocus our sessions with Ashley. We needed to lead her differently – not through convincing her or persuading her, but instead we had to acknowledge where we went wrong, what was missing in our leadership strategy, and reset with a refocused strategy of small, consistent and intentional fragments of positive exposure of the initiative through the "Meerkat Effect".

The Meerkat Effect will be discussed in detail in Chapter 10 and is referenced throughout this book as an essential part of the success of the SKIM Model. The Meerkat Effect is the space in which you and your team continuously and transparently discuss, celebrate, model, build the vision, create the momentum, and drive the positive energy in the improvement process. Done well, the Meerkat Effect is like a snowball, gathering speed down a steep mountain – slow to start with but gradually picking up speed, size, force and impact. It is like a meerkat standing at its post, on top of its burrow, scanning with curiosity, wondering what is going on in the distance. Your staff will be curious and naturally will want to be a part of the successful improvement strategy. The Meerkat Effect is not a tool used to "convince" or "persuade" your staff to engage; it is a process of building momentum through small, purposeful, intentional snippets of positive exposure to the improvement implementation process.

The 3Cs are supported by an article by Dellaert and Davydov (2017) for the Centre for Creative Leadership, which discusses three key elements that influence those you lead – the head, the heart, and the hands:

- The head – focusing on appealing to the individual's intellectual understanding: the research, the evidence, the direction, the desired outcome.
- The heart – appealing to the emotional connection: the staff member's beliefs and values and their individual, professional and personal goals.
- The hands – appealing to the individual's collaborative needs and the feeling of inclusion and consultation within a team or group of staff.

We had been confident with our influence on the head and the hands leadership in the writing initiative, but with this staff member we had missed the opportunity to influence the heart, which impacted the credibility of the Success Team's process.

We knew the destination of the area for improvement (selecting the right stone), we had set the agenda and started at the first skim, Success. However, what was a small, missed leadership opportunity meant a larger challenge to get this staff member realigned with our improvement agenda. Breakspear and Ryrie Jones argue that "once we know the destination (the goal), it is helpful to recognise that it is not ambition that will get us there, but thoughtful mapping of small evidence-informed improvement, worked on over time, in a way that is sustainable, and perhaps even pleasurable. It's important to remember that motivation often emerges as an outcome of making progress, not the other way around" (2020, p. 41). Slowly but surely, we led the Success Team member to have a greater understanding of the initiative's intentions and we were able to gain their support through positive examples and experiences that began to be seen as an achievable and enjoyable learning practice for teachers and ultimately their students.

Discussion

Choosing the Success Team is arguably the most valuable and intentional decision you will make, beyond selecting the right stone. This is not because this team is any more important than the rest of your staff, but rather because the Success Team will set the tone for the momentum you will build early in the implementation of your improvement agenda. Success as it is defined is simply about achieving your goals, aims or what you have intended to do. That is the purpose of this team. They will not achieve the improvement by themselves; however, through implementing the Meerkat Effect strategy, the Knowledge, Inquisitive and Measured Teams will be eagerly watching. Their perception of the initiative will be created by observing their peers' or colleagues' successes. Although I discussed the staff member I selected for my Success Team, I did not consider an element in their cultural beliefs that impacted their engagement with the improvement focus area. This was not a failed attempt to implement the SKIM Model. They could still have been the right choice for the team; we simply did not select the right strategy for leading them. The remainder of the team were still leading the positive implementation, and for the challenging staff member we simply had to adjust our leadership strategy.

The size of every Success Team I have selected has varied according to my leadership team's 3Cs assessment of the staff we were leading, the resources we had, the size of the improvement agenda, the capacity of my staff, and the overall strategy I wanted to employ in leading. However, always remember that we are playing the long game, so less is best. Using the Meerkat Effect (discussed in Chapter 10), you will be able to invest your energy in "the few", who will quickly become "the many".

The decisions you are making today will not have an impact until tomorrow. Remember, it is a perceived race, but the only team that is competing for the win is you and your staff. Do it slow and do it well.

Leadership reflection task

Select one of your pending/future improvement strategies or initiatives. Refer to Figure 6 – The 3Cs.

- ☐ Which staff do you believe would be the right (not the easy) staff to begin the SKIM Model with?
- ☐ Have you experienced a "get it wrong moment" when leading improvement?
- ☐ What was/is your reflection on why it did not work?
- ☐ If you were in this position again, how would you lead differently?

Success Team – Quick take-aways

- ✓ Plan and be intentional in your approach and strategy.
- ✓ The first lead team are the team all other staff are carefully watching. Use the Meerkat Effect (Chapter 10) effectively to celebrate, showcase and build capacity and momentum across your whole staff.
- ✓ Select the right team, not the easy team. The easy team will be on board either way. Focus attention on getting the next level of engagement from those that are on the cusp of getting on board early.
- ✓ Use the 3Cs to support staff engagement (see page 60). Intentionally plan how you are going to lead improvement and who are going to be your Success Team leading the way.
- ✓ This team's success will build the momentum for the Knowledge Team. Don't hide failure or challenge – this is part of improvement. Instead celebrate the challenge and work as a collaborative team to identify and overcome anything that is preventing or distracting from the end goal of improvement.

CHAPTER 7
Knowledge

Figure 7: The SKIM Model: Knowledge

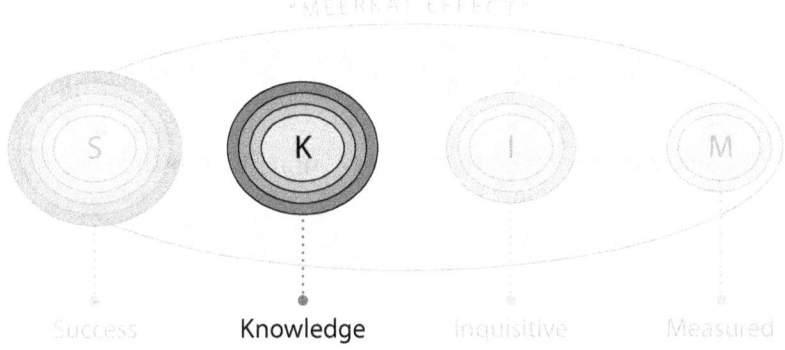

For the purpose of understanding the SKIM Model, we focus on the idea of "knowledge" as a person who values, appreciates and seeks out information, understanding or insight into a topic of an improvement area. The person is led by a level of curiosity and has a strong desire to learn and acquire additional evidence or details of an improvement area before proceeding. They have a level of hesitation about the focus area or may have a belief that there is an increased risk to them as an individual or as a professional. Overall, a staff member who is sitting in the knowledge ripple places high importance on intellectual development and understanding, knowing that this knowledge will empower them to be successful in the pursuit of improvement.

The Knowledge Team will observe the accomplishments of the Success Team with a great deal of weight and significance. The Success Team will naturally become teacher leaders; as Gardner (1993) argues, every great teacher is a leader. Their work will be the basis for the Knowledge Team to gain confidence to take on the next stage of the improvement process. I will refer again to the impact the "Meerkat Effect" (Chapter 10) will have in building the Knowledge Team's understanding, capacity and confidence in joining the improvement journey.

As a leader in any organisation, it is essential that you build the capacity of your team to support and lead the work at every level from identification through to implementation of an improvement agenda. Dinham, in his book *How to Get Your School Moving and Improving* (2011), suggests that great leaders understand and recognise that for any improvement to be established and become part of the organisation's culture, there needs to be a significant amount of trust in the people you lead. This trust is then supported through distributed responsibilities and leadership opportunities. The SKIM Model is based on a distributive leadership model. The Knowledge Team will be the next group of staff to support and lead the improvement focus area. They will have an influence (positive or negative) on the SKIM teams that will follow.

Every experienced leader was once a young leader

If I reflect on my leadership career so far, it has evolved and the continuum of where my "default" position is within the SKIM Model has also evolved. Although everyone's position within the SKIM Model (Success, Knowledge, Inquisitive or Measured) can vary throughout their career, based on many factors, we all have a default, a fall-back position. When things are equal or we are in a position of cognitive overload, there would be a stage within any model or framework that would be our comfortable or common position. I believe my personal default would be the Knowledge Team. This has changed over the years, and I can recall early in my leadership when I would have squarely sat in the Success Team space. I can recall many occasions where I have had a member of the central office team or wider community call and make me an offer to be involved in an event, a new initiative, an excursion, and many other great opportunities. The young, Success Team me was a bit of a "Yeah, why not?" kind of a leader – say yes now and work out the process later. I had a high level of trust in the people leading me, so I accepted the endorsement of those who were offering numerous opportunities.

However, as I have gained more experience and curiosity, my leadership has also evolved. I would comfortably say that the system leaders that led me as a principal, using the SKIM Model, would arguably place me in the Knowledge Team as well. I am highly motivated by the "why". Simon Sinek (2009), in his text *Start with Why: How Great Leaders Inspire Everyone to Take Action*, argues that leaders do not inspire people by "what" they do or even "how" they do their role. Sinek argues that people buy into a leader's ideas and motivations by understanding "why" they do what they do. I have always had a desire to understand the evidence of impact, to get a gauge from other organisations that have implemented an initiative, and to understand the influence this strategy or event may have had on the organisation. I need to know this before committing. If the pressure is on with a short timeline, and I have not accessed the needed details, then my fallback response would be, "No, I don't think this is for us right now."

We must acknowledge that our staff, like you and I, are also influenced by their own personal experiences and gain understanding over their careers and personal lives. In saying that, we then need to ensure this does not create an unfair or unsupported bias when we are leading our team. As you move through the SKIM Model, you will see that no skim places the people you are leading in a deficit position. No skim is more important than the other. Success holds a level of importance in getting the momentum; however, you need to accept that the people are responding based on their needs and understandings, and your leadership is an essential part of getting them engaged with your process. You will find a level of peace and enjoyment in the process, a calmness that allows you to focus on the right work with the right people in the right way.

Hargreaves and Fullan, in their book *Professional Capital: Transforming Teaching in Every School* (2012), argue that teachers go through three stages in their careers:

1. Early (enthusiasm is great but capability is low)
2. Mid (enthusiasm and capability are both high and balanced)
3. Late (enthusiasm is less than capability, so they become cynical).

Munby (2019) suggests that this could also apply to leaders. However, it is a perspective that Munby challenges, as do I. This simplistic view suggests we all have a point in our career where we are at our peak performance, and then we start to decline and roll down the hill into our eventual retirement. I would argue this is a cynical view of our adult learners and undervalues the experience and knowledge our later-career teachers and leaders provide.

Some of the greatest teachers I have worked with were in the later parts of their careers. In one of my earliest team-teaching roles, I was moved from a senior class to a junior, and to say I was not excited was an understatement. Trudi, my team teacher, was extremely experienced and, as it turned out, had grown up in the same era as my dad in a small Victorian country town and knew some of Dad's family. My level of enthusiasm was low based on how I had chosen to view the change of year levels. Referring to Hargreaves and Fullan's view, my capability was also low – I had only been in education for a short time. However, I look back at the two years I taught with Trudi as some of my fondest, along with the fact that I had to lift my enthusiasm to attempt to elevate it to the same level as Trudi's, which was high.

I have also led many graduates, who I would agree come into the profession with high levels of enthusiasm; however, I would argue that their capability and capacity for learning and thriving ran rings around some of our "mid-career" educators. If we accept that we have a "peak" in our careers, we are running a significant risk of pigeon-holing staff into categories that may unfairly represent them and can change, based on motivation and, more importantly, the leadership. I am sure you have all come across students who were considered the "naughty" ones. They were aware of this opinion; you were aware that they were aware. So, what did they do? They did not let you down and lived up to the expectations of being the naughty ones. However, this can change; we can break the cycle when we have unconditional positive regard. They are not really the "naughty" ones – they simply need different strategies and approaches. It is not an overnight process, but it works. I am now asking you to consider the same with the people you lead: unconditional positive regard. Open the possibility of leading them differently, without bias or an opinion of what they "might" do. Change the approach or strategies. Change the way you lead.

The SKIM Model is built on the idea that your staff will respond to you as a leader when they are ready. Being "ready" is not indefinite; there is a timeline that you need to set, and you will see this as you move through the SKIM Model. It is, however, our role to find the currency and motivations of our staff. Sharratt, in her book *Clarity*, suggests that "sustaining the work is about breaking the mindset that, 'I am the expert and I need to know all the answers' and moving humbly to an inquiry stance, 'How do we together, accomplish success for all?'" (2019, p. 303). Good leadership is about having confidence in the goals, aims and objectives of the improvement agenda, while being open and receptive to the views of others. It is about setting up a culture where robust, respectful challenge is encouraged and considered as part of the improvement process. Young me often saw challenge when a staff member communicated to me that they did not agree with what I was suggesting, as if this also implied that they did not respect my leadership. In essence, I had to get over myself. It is not about me; it is about the best decision that is going to have the best outcome for our organisation and the people in it. It is my privilege as the leader to build the culture, through open leadership where we accept the differences in others, acknowledge positive intent, and adjust leadership to support the people we lead. Not everyone will require the same considerations for their success in this team or any others in the SKIM Model.

I do remember how I was made to feel

The SKIM Model is a positive approach that leads with the strong belief that everyone has positive intent and simply requires a different leadership approach. But what if a staff member genuinely doesn't have positive intent? This is a great question and one we will discuss in Chapter 12.

Every element of the SKIM Model is based on motivation through positive exposure and experience. This is key to the success of the model, and the benefits of positive engagement are deeply embedded in research.

Munby argues that a culture that relies entirely on motivation through fear and challenge can only take leaders so far, and its positive aspects are short-lived (2019, p. 153). He goes on to argue that whenever you set targets or lay down criteria for success and make the consequence of success or failure overly significant, people will focus on those things to the detriment of other things.

I recall a moment in my early leadership days when I had a very short but significant conversation with a senior leader. To be honest, it was probably an arbitrary few sentences that held no significance for the senior leader, but did to me. I remember how it made me feel, and that it highlighted the importance of giving appropriate feedback, celebrating other people's efforts, and acknowledging opinions differing to my own.

I had been asked to develop a staff induction booklet, a document we did not have, and one that we deemed important for staff consistency and the dissemination of important policy, governance and process. We had employed a few new staff, so this booklet was going to be trialled with the newest members of the team at the start of the following year. I got into the task and gathered some different examples from similar environments. After a few weeks, I had completed the first draft – approximately 20 pages of information to support new and existing teachers. I was proud of my efforts and of the document, although I knew there would be some things I had missed. My next step was to share this with some of my colleagues and obtain feedback. They came back to me with some great suggestions regarding changes, things I had forgotten to include, and irrelevant things I could omit. Finally, it was time to present the draft to my direct manager. I proudly walked into her office, placed it on her desk, and said "Draft one complete", with a smile on my face. I explained the thorough process I had been through to get to this point and asked for her feedback.

About three days later, my manager walked into my office, dropped the draft on my desk, said it needed to be redone, and started to walk out. "Sorry, what part?" I asked, confused. "All of it – it's not what I want," she replied. I sat perplexed for a while, with fury building up inside me. Effort, process, time, creativity – I felt none of these had been acknowledged or respected. With a simple few words, I had been cut down, and younger me had taken it quite personally. I picked the book up and walked into my manager's office.

In an assertive voice I asked directly, "What exactly do you not like – what needs to change?" My manager repeated, "All of it." I dropped the draft on her desk and said, "I am not changing all of it. I will email you a copy, and if you want to give me some specific feedback to consider I will change it. Otherwise you can create a new one."

It is almost two decades on, and this simple example sticks with me. Why? I don't exactly know. It may be because it was the first time I stood up and said "I do not agree with your approach" to a superior or because I genuinely thought I deserved some more credit for my efforts. Either way, I remember it like it was yesterday. This memory ensures that I spend a lot of time appreciating the efforts of other people, rather than focusing on whether the completed document is perfect or could be improved. The staff member has put in effort that needs to be acknowledged first and foremost.

When leading any improvement process, even the creation of a staff induction booklet, if the process is not heading in a direction that is as favourable as I and my leadership team had anticipated, I reflect firstly on myself:

- Did I communicate the parameters of the improvement process effectively?
- Do my teams understand the direction?
- Does the staff member who created the induction booklet (for example) have positive intent to support the people within the organisation?

After reflecting on the questions above, if the teams have deviated from the plan and still have positive intent, it is highly probably that it is us, the leaders, who need to change the process or communication, to bring the initiative back on track and align the team. Our staff, in the vast majority of cases, are doing what they think is right, with positive intent and contributing individual effort, time, creativity and pride. Appreciate and acknowledge your teams, then get to work on what decisions or changes you need to make as the leader to ensure you are back on track.

What does it look like if I get it right?

I am now going to flip my reflection on the Knowledge Team and talk about what this team will look like if you get it right. The purpose of this is to highlight that your Knowledge Team will be impacted heavily by the momentum built by your Success Team – as your Inquisitive Team will be influenced by your Knowledge Team and your Measured Team will be carefully watching the Inquisitive Team to build their confidence and enthusiasm. As the SKIM Model visual represents, all of this has the Meerkat Effect wrapped around it, which will have a significant influence on the positive engagement of all elements of the SKIM Model. As Defour and Fullan suggest, a catalyst for motivation is a sense of progress in overcoming a challenge or achieving a goal (2013, p. 73).

There are several approaches you can implement to recruit your Knowledge Team, some of which can happen naturally through the effective implementation of the SKIM Model. However, remember that hope is not a strategy, so considered planning about the next members of your teams is imperative – you cannot hope that the team will form naturally.

1. **Pre-considered** – As a leadership team, you might "pencil in" a couple of the staff that are on the cusp of the Success Team. They might be people you know simply need a little bit of time to process but generally are early to engage with new initiatives. You might have a few that you were considering for the Success Team; however, after reflecting on "Context, Capacity, Culture" (Figure 6), you and your leadership team decided to give them a little more time before engaging them. Please note: I said "pencil in" rather than "ink in". The SKIM Model is a continuum, and you don't want to make assumptions. So, one of the staff you "pencilled in" still may not be ready to engage in the Knowledge Team.

2. **Volunteering** – Your Success Team may naturally build the confidence of a staff member you hadn't considered at that point. They may be a team member whose curiosity has been sparked and who is keen to get involved as a learner. Having a differentiated approach is still essential. The pace this staff member may need could be significantly different to that of the other members. I am of the belief that if a staff member wants to learn, I am not going to stand in their way – bring it on and embrace it.

3. **Natural selection** – This is not the same as Darwin's theory of natural selection, but you may have a staff member that has started dabbling

in the improvement focus area with some of the information they have been able to access in their adult learning sessions or through observations or conversations with a colleague. They may have talked to some of the Success Team or asked for a little more information that they want to consider. If the staff member is keen and taking the lead, this shows that your SKIM Model implementation has been effective, but also what a great culture of adult learning you have, if your staff are wanting to be a part of improvement and are leading their own development in the focus area.

Discussion

Defour and Fullan (2013), in *Cultures Built to Last*, argue that early in any change process people will act out of compliance rather than commitment and that commitment will only emerge after tangible results can be seen. It is these tangible results, coupled with positive examples of success, that will move the "fence sitters" among your staff from compliance to genuinely supporting and advocating for the change. The SKIM Model is a process, one that should be carefully considered and not rushed. Each ripple in the SKIM Model leads to the next. We have established that in education there will always be this feeling of perceived urgency – I doubt the pace will slow. As the leader, you can choose to slow down or speed up implementation. Although it often doesn't feel like it, you are in complete control of that. Approach the implementation of the SKIM Model with the "get it right rather than get it done" approach and watch the culture continue to thrive.

Dinham (2011) found through his research that schools that are thriving are being led by leaders that have a positive attitude to change. They do not see change as a threat and are open to an opportunity. How a leader responds to the pressures of change is being examined by your staff. Positive modelling is important: demonstrating how you want your staff to react to any improvement or change, even when it is mandated. This is the first step to starting the momentum or stalling it.

The Knowledge Team is not a fixed group; the context, the environment, and the number of people you are leading will determine the composition of the team. Each effective SKIM Model will look slightly different. The size of each of your teams will be determined by how many you need to make sure you have a positive impact and can keep the momentum going. However, size is not as important as the people who are in it; their engagement will drive the next ripples in the SKIM Model.

Leadership reflection task

Answer the following questions:

- ☐ Why do you do what you do as a leader?
- ☐ As a team, create a set of norms that reflect "Why is your organisation better having you as their leadership team?"
- ☐ Why do you do what you do as a team?

Knowledge Team – Quick take-aways

- ✓ Actively watch the Success Teams to build their understanding and capacity to engage. Through both informal and formal conversations (professional teams/collaborative planning/professional learning) and the Meerkat Effect (Chapter 10), the Knowledge Team will be building their confidence to engage.
- ✓ It will not take a lot of energy to engage in the improvement strategy. The Knowledge Team will most likely be reasonably obvious as the next staff to get on board. However, it is important to be intentional in your selection. This team will influence your Inquisitive Team; engage the right staff that will support the momentum of the next step in your improvement process.
- ✓ They may naturally join the team, or be selected or volunteer to engage in the improvement strategy.
- ✓ As you lead this team, you will need to reflect on the next steps of engagement. The decision you make here and through the Meerkat Effect will be a significant support as you progress.

CHAPTER 8

Inquisitive

Figure 8: The SKIM Model: Inquisitive

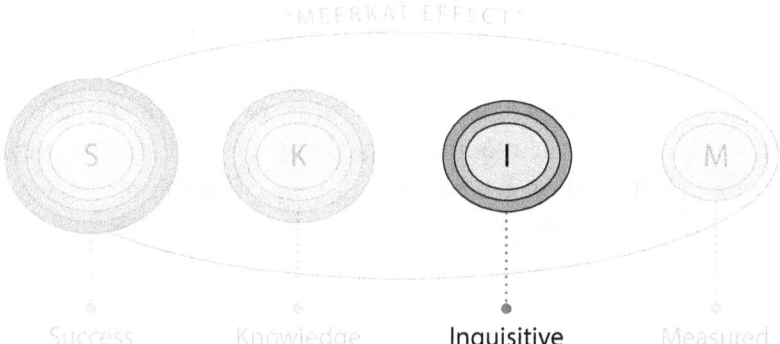

Like all dispositions, we could portray an inquisitive person in many diverse ways, depending on the subject we are discussing. Within the SKIM Model, the "Inquisitive Team" is one that has several key characteristics aligned to the general definitions of being inquisitive; however, some of the attributes that can be seen when leading improvement may occasionally be perceived as stubborn or rigid. That is, the techniques this team uses to find information may be seen as challenging or even at times argumentative. As I discussed in the previous chapter, the SKIM Model is about positive intent, leading with an open mind and adjusting your intentional leadership strategies to get the best out of the staff you are leading. As Munby (2019) argues, when people in our organisations are acting in undesirable ways, it is important that we look at ourselves as leaders and consider whether our own processes or leadership behaviours are promoting or encouraging these staff to act this way. Leading people is not a static skill, and when we are talking about leading improvement, our staff will not stumble across the desired destination by accident or as a coincidence. This must be planned with a genuine focus on what we need to do as the leader to build the confidence and capacity in our staff and ultimately have the greatest impact in every learning environment.

Being inquisitive is characterised by being curious. An inquisitive person endeavours to increase their understanding of a topic through conversations, observations, research, data or professional reading. They often have the tendency to ask questions and pursue answers. In addition to this, inquisitive people are often not satisfied with broad, general or suspected superficial answers. These types of generic answers will often have an adverse effect on their engagement and will increase their potential challenge or rigidity. Like all adult learners, the Inquisitive Team's initial thinking is "How will this perceived change impact me?" As Guskey argues, substantial adjustment in teachers' beliefs and dispositions towards a change or improvement agenda will only occur after there has been evidence of improved outcomes (1983, p. 58). By the time you are beginning your focused approach with the Inquisitive Team, you will have evidence to discuss and small improvements to celebrate.

Macklin and Zbar (2020) argue that leaders often spend a significant amount of their time focusing on the staff that are late starters, investing a lot of energy in attempts to lead these staff to positively engage in an improvement strategy. However, there is often little return for the amount of energy invested. The SKIM Model gives you permission to be OK with accepting your staff for who they are and what they bring to your team, and accepting that they will engage at different times along the continuum. I will argue that this permission will alleviate a level of stress and reduce the investment of energy in a place where you will get little gain initially. If you follow the SKIM Model, your energy will be fully invested in momentum. The late starters will not have been let off the hook with your improvement agenda, but rather you will be leading a differentiated approach that will provide opportunity and bounded choice. The result will be a consistent whole-staff approach and engagement in ongoing improvement.

The formation of the Inquisitive Team is a significant milestone in your improvement leadership. Like the ripples of the skimming stone, this group is slightly smaller than the last. They have been active participants in the ongoing professional learning and evidence-based celebrations through the Meerkat Effect. They know the direction and by this time they have a good understanding of the improvement agenda, its purpose, and the desired outcome. They have started to see this in action with real, context-based examples and evidence. So, will this be easy? Sorry to burst your bubble, but the group may be smaller and have had a lot of exposure, but your leadership is just as important and strategic as it has been through the initial stages of the SKIM Model. The work you have been doing prior to the Inquisitive Team has been setting the foundations, ensuring the footings are solid and safe. Now we need to build the frame before we can put the roof on.

The Inquisitive Team is the space where I personally get high levels of motivation and inspiration in leading improvement. I know that when we have engaged this team in the initiative, our organisation has put high-quality, effective leadership skills to the test. Through the initial steps in the SKIM Model (Success and Knowledge), what you have effectively built is an extension of your leadership team. Your leadership team has increased, and the Success and Knowledge Teams are now in a position to support the leading of the improvement agenda. I like to refer to this process as "leadership that leads leaders to lead". These initial teams are now the ambassadors of the initiative or focus area. You have a greater support network around you. Defour and Fullan have explained that "when an organisation has created widespread ownership of the change process and developed the leadership potential of its members, people throughout the organisation take collective responsibility for preserving its culture" (2013, p. 72).

We cannot underestimate the significance of the relationship of the people we are leading in the Success and Knowledge Teams as well as the Inquisitive and Measured Teams. The SKIM Model is a set of processes that cannot overshadow your role in developing relationships through leadership. Dinham argues that "successful change is more about active leadership of people than management of systems" (2011, p. 128). Implementing an effective SKIM Model will, like a classroom instructional model, enable you to have the cognitive capacity to focus on the people within your organisation. The Inquisitive Team need that focus and genuine engagement to meet their specific adult learning needs. Investing time in your people will pay dividends in your leadership processes. When leading improvement, one of the key opportunities for senior leadership and their leadership team is to continue to assess what the obstacles are that potentially could slow or restrict the momentum. Defour and Fullan (2013) highlight that demonstrating mutual accountability in minimising obstacles through leadership of an initiative is heavily based and reliant on ongoing communication, not only when the improvement initiative has been launched, but all the way through the implementation process.

As you begin to narrow its outcome, you now have only a small number of staff that are required to engage in the improvement strategy. The selection of the Inquisitive Team can be an essential ingredient for the success of the final team (the Measured Team). As with our initial steps, the Inquisitive Team is not different – we must be intentional in our process and strategy. I will again repeat that we must focus on the right people, not the easy people. The last thing you want to do is build your Inquisitive Team with an unintentional outcome of ostracising the final few staff to come on board – the "naughty staff" discussed earlier.

A great prompt question to support your process with the Inquisitive Team could be:

Which of the remaining staff are going to have the most positive influence on the Measured Team?

This question will support in identifying your "deliberate/influential" staff selection (discussed later in this chapter). You will firstly need to consider the 3Cs, then whether they may be a confidant of one of the Measured Team members. They may be a mentor, team teacher or trusted colleague. They may need strong leadership to get them on the improvement bus; however, you know that if you lead them to engage in the initiative the next process in the SKIM Model will be just that little bit smoother. Again, they may be perceived as tricky or on the cusp of the Measured Team, but let's never forget that if we base our expectations on assumptions, like the "naughty kid", we may be setting ourselves and our staff up for failure. Who is going to have the greatest positive influence on the remaining staff? That is a great question to bring to your Inquisitive Team process.

There are staff in every organisation that have built the profile of being difficult, and sometimes it can seem like they have a direct vendetta or agenda they are wanting to achieve with their negativity. There is a process for the small percentage of staff in our system that genuinely fit into this category (discussed in Chapter 12). However, I do not believe I have ever come across a staff member who has woken up, looked in the mirror, and said, "Today I am going to have a terrible day." The vast majority of staff members that I have worked with enter the work environment not wanting conflict or disputes; nonetheless, there are some that disputes seem to find.

It is helpful to remember that our teachers are committed to the things they teach. As Palmer puts it, "the things I teach are things I care about – and what I care about helps define selfhood" (1998, p. 17). The narrative that we enter any situation with, whether professionally or personally, will always have a biased position that is in our own favour. This is neither right nor wrong; it is human nature. Knight (2011) argues that staff often – to protect their self-esteem – will over time develop a narrative that explains why they are not achieving their goals. Knight suggests that some of the narrative may have a level of truth – for example, students' lack of motivation, parents' lack of support, heavy curriculum, interruptions to learning, and so on. These may have an impact at some level; however, as the staff member embeds these beliefs and their narrative becomes their reality, every comment or feedback we provide as a leader or colleague can be taken personally.

As a leader, it is in our best interests to gain an understanding of each of our staff's personal narrative, so we can best support them to add value to it through consideration of how an improvement strategy might enhance the things they care about and not undermine their values and beliefs. As a leader, in order to have balanced dialogue, it is essential to take a step back, regulate emotions, listen objectively and understand, not necessarily to respond. Bringing your team into your calm through active communication, rather than joining some of the team members in their emotional response, is essential to ensure the success of all staff.

Sharratt suggests that successful leaders hold their nerve, make small pivots along the way, trust their team "with noble intent" and directly deal with and resolve conflict as it appears (2019, p. 306). Importantly, these leaders are part of the learning, not separate to it. They can provide autonomy to their team and balance this out with appropriate levels of direction, support and accountability. When we are challenged, we are learning. We see this in our classrooms with students daily; we see this in our staff meetings with the responses of our adult learners to new learning. I experience challenges as a leader daily in so many facets of my role, and I find if there is ever a fleeting moment where I am in a "challenge lull" I soon begin seeking re-entry into the challenge space. This is what has often led leaders to leadership roles. There is a drive for new learning and finding solutions to problems or challenges.

Munby (2019) argues that as we lead, the secret is not to reduce the challenges that our teams face. Instead, he suggests that our staff want a job that challenges them and that we as leaders should model an open and engaging style that welcomes and acknowledges challenges for our teams to see. I talked earlier about "removing obstacles" to support the momentum of learning with our teams; I want to be clear that "challenge" is not an obstacle that we want to remove. Challenge is learning, and learning is challenge; we need to create the appropriate learning culture where this is accepted as a certainty rather than an obstacle. We should lead with an assurance that we will resource, support, problem-solve and collaborate to overcome challenges, but we will not avoid them.

In Chapter 6, I discussed a leadership blooper with Ashley that our team did not get right. We had not considered Ashley's core beliefs in teaching and learning. The reality was that within that scenario Ashley would have most likely fit into the Inquisitive Team better than the Success Team. She needed more exposure to the theory of practice, the research, the structure, the evidence or outcomes, to see that this improvement was adding value to her already strong love of writing. I like to compare this with pushing a beach ball under water – eventually the pressure is going to force the beach ball into the air. Similarly, with Ashley, we went into Success Team mode straightaway and sent her flying (figuratively) because we had not considered her holistic needs as an adult learner. Understanding how your staff learn and what they need to be successful will ensure that, as you head into each of the skim ripples, you will enjoy the successes of your team rather than lament the decisions of engaging this team or staff member in the improvement process. If you think about achieving the result, you must lead and positively engage every member of your team, but not at the same time. As McCauley and Van Velsor (2004) argue, for any organisation to engage in sustained leadership of improvement, it needs more than simply well-developed individuals. Just as important are the well-developed relationships that are based on an aligned focus on shared work.

When I was in the early stages of developing the skeleton of the SKIM Model – although I hadn't built a visual representation, or the language to support and explain the process – I can remember one of the first instances where I implemented intentional strategies to lead a team member, while struggling to understand what was driving his motivation. Over a few years, I had come to learn that James was an adult learner who needed time. He needed understanding of concepts, research and purpose. He often verbalised questions that sounded like a child learning the ways of the world: "But why? But why?" I remember younger me often feeling frustrated with the constant questioning, when other staff members were able to – at least on the surface – accept the discussion and direction and trot off to have a go. When I reflect now, James' default learning space in the SKIM Model was the Inquisitive Team. He was not actively trying to be difficult; he just needed something different to my other team members in order to embrace the improvement focus area.

There is no denying that people in every organisation respond and react in vastly diverse ways to any change or improvement agenda, due to the culture, pressure, individual perspective, beliefs or values, leadership, perceived competency of oneself – I could go on listing. As Dinham argues, the "culture and climate of the organisation and the experience and views of individuals and groups within it towards change will be important in determining reactions and responses to change, responses which can be both emotional and behavioral" (2011, p. 120). Dinham goes on to list some of the possible predispositions that staff may have towards change:

- See change as a threat to their power base, responsibility, or autonomy.
- Feel uneasy about the risk and possible failures associated with the change.

- Be deterred by the pressure to "do more with less" or even with the same resources.
- Feel undervalued or devalued by what is being proposed.
- Find potential disruptions to established procedures and even traditions threatening (2011, p. 120).

I would argue that many of the above responses are not only predictable but also preventable, by knowing your staff as adult learners and leading them appropriately. As a leader, I often hear colleagues discussing such responses, and although debriefing with trusting colleagues is an important part of any leadership, I question why we tend to want to push back against our staff's perceived negative responses. We know these are part of human nature and embedded as deeply valued beliefs; with that knowledge we also must acknowledge that simply wanting our staff to "toe the line" and "get on board" will not be sufficient. Learning the default dispositions of your staff and planning to lead with that knowledge empowers you as a leader to make strong, confident decisions. We can never prevent such responses; in fact, I do not believe it is healthy not to have these challenges in my staff room. As discussed above, we need and will thrive with challenge. However, with knowledge comes power, and the power you use in preparing for your individual staff needs will mean you can lessen the energy expended on staff responses that "catch you by surprise". You will have predicted a level of behaviours or emotions, and you can begin accepting these as your staff members' response to challenge, their learning pit that you can lead them out of over time. Again, I do not want to confuse these responses with poor behaviour or dispositions that must be addressed through a different process. I am talking about the responses that you and I and all our staff will make based on Dinham's list above and many more variables such as assumed human behaviours and emotions.

The Inquisitive Team's beginning

It was the start of the new school year and many of my staff had not moved classes or classrooms for several years. I was never one to move staff for the sake of moving; however, I knew that with an increase in predicted enrolments for the following year, coupled with a retirement, we would need some new staff and some changes to our learning environments. I had to make some changes to the current structure and had seen that there were several year level changes that I was going to have to enact with my teaching staff to get the right balance of knowledge and experience. One of these changes that needed to take place was moving James from a senior class (Year 7) to a junior class (Year 1). From my previous experience, and having gained a greater understanding and appreciation of what James needed to be a successful adult learner, I knew this change would be difficult for James, particularly without a significant amount of lead time to ensure that he had all the information he needed to be successful. Ultimately, if James entered this experience with the wrong outlook, it would be the students that would be mostly impacted.

James had only ever taught senior primary and junior secondary school, and on his yearly consultation opportunity to provide his preference for the following year's class, it was cut and paste from year to year:

- Option 1: Year 7
- Option 2: Year 6
- Option 3: Year 5/6

With this information, I thought I would attempt a different approach. I could not straight out say to James in February, "In 12 months I might be moving you to a Year 1 class" and list off the reasons why. Apart from the fact that this might cause possible conflict and questions from other staff that I did not have answers for, the other issue was that this was based on predicted numbers, and things could change.

My approach was not complex, but I was focusing on the "long, slow game" of leadership. The initial step in building James' confidence was to expose him to small, planned, purposeful positive interactions with this year level. After setting up a meeting with James and the current Year 1 team leader, we decided to develop a buddy system that would support our student leadership and personal and interpersonal development while also presenting James with opportunities to develop relationships and an understanding of the Year 1 students. My next strategy was to support James with understanding the curriculum of the year level. At the time, we were focusing on improving our curriculum planner's consistency and detail across the school. Utilising this improvement agenda, I asked James and his senior teaching team to collaborate with several of the junior teams during the consultation and development phase. This had an impact on the whole-school approach to consistency, with an intentional approach to support James with his understanding of the junior school planning processes and curriculum.

Throughout the year, there were many more opportunistic decisions where we found small positive engagement opportunities for James and the junior team or students. At the end of the year, as per normal, I started our consultative approach to teachers' placement for the following year, where I ask for preferences and any possible leave or other considerations from each of my staff. I waited for James' response with anticipation. It was:

- Option 1: Year 7
- Option 2: Year 6
- Option 3: Year 1

Although James had selected Year 1 as his final preference, he came to see me to make a point, "only if I am really needed in the junior team". James wanted to feel that his expertise and what he could offer the junior team was "needed" or valued. We were in a position where everyone was a winner. It was still going to be an adjustment, and we still needed to support James; however, we had a lot to celebrate. If this had fallen through, as a school we would not have lost out, and James was not in a position where he had committed to any particular outcome. Our students still had developed strong skills through the buddy system, and our staff had benefited from the cross-level collaboration.

I am not suggesting that the Inquisitive Team requires 12 months of strategic leadership to get on board. However, they will, as with every team, need specific planning and individualised approaches to support their engagement. The Inquisitive Team want to engage; they simply need your strong leadership and a differentiated adult learning approach to support their understanding and commitment.

Who is inquisitive?

This is a good question and one that does not have any one answer. There are a few possible directions that you can adjust to build your Inquisitive Team. The first for all the SKIM Model teams is to refer to your individual knowledge, with a particular focus on Figure 6 (p. 60) and the prompt questions for "Context, Culture and Capacity". However, you are now starting to get the minority of your staff on board, so the selection can become a little more intentional. How your Inquisitive Team might present themselves to you could be based on many factors; one and often the most important is a leader's knowledge of their staff. Some of the alternative categories that often present are:

1. **Natural selection and volunteering** – As discussed in the previous chapter, both categories will continue to present themselves as you activate your staff members' confidence and excitement about the opportunities. The Inquisitive Team is inquisitive, so if you build their knowledge and understanding you will get greater momentum. Natural selection will see staff engage with genuine curiosity. If you have an interested staff member wanting to learn, embrace it.

2. **Deliberate/influential selection** – After the Inquisitive Team, you have only the Measured Team remaining to finalise the implementation of your improvement agenda. The deliberate/influential selection allows you to harness the influence of your remaining staff before embarking on the final process in the SKIM Model. Consider any staff that are on the cusp of your Inquisitive Team and your Measured Team. These selections would be staff that are likely to have a positive influence on the remaining staff. They may be in the same team as or be a confidant colleague to one or a few of your remaining staff. Building their capacity and positive influence will get you a few steps closer to engaging the Measured Team without focusing on or directing excess energy to this last group of the SKIM Model.

Discussion

Tracey Ezard, in her book *Ferocious Warmth*, explains that the most inspiring leaders are those who are still explicitly learning their craft, still making mistakes, trying new things, reflecting and adjusting (2021, p. 22). As a leader, you are continuously modelling how to manage change and improvement, how to react to ambiguity, curiosity and challenge. I personally have learnt more about being a leader through leading – getting it right, getting it wrong – but most importantly either way, reflecting on why the result or outcome eventuated. Our Inquisitive Team thrive on the same success and achievements as we do as the leaders of our organisations. Our challenge is to see the improvement barriers from their perspective and support them to see around, through or past these barriers. We have the power to decide how we interpret the Inquisitive Team's curiosity, how we respond and reflect on our approach. If we approach each team with an authentic learning-based approach and harness their questions to better serve the improvement strategy through deeper investigations, clarifying discussions or broadening our research breadth and depth, the outcome can only be a better implementation, a greater impact, and a more committed team with a superior improvement outcome at the end.

Leadership reflection task

Selecting one of your current improvement strategies or processes:

- ☐ What have been some of the identified barriers in your process/strategy?
- ☐ How have you led/supported to minimise the impact of these barriers on the improvement process/strategy?
- ☐ Are there others you have possibly overlooked or categorised as an individual's issue rather than a barrier to continuing the momentum of the improvement process?
- ☐ What pre-planning can you consider for potential barriers in other areas of improvement?

Inquisitive Team – Quick take-aways

✓ Strong evidence is needed to build their interest in engaging. The Inquisitive Team have now been observing the Success Team and the Knowledge Team through different forums such as (but not limited to) professional teams/collaborative planning/professional learning and holistically the effective use of the Meerkat Effect in your professional adult learning or incidentally in your collaborative team planning sessions.

- ✓ They might have strong beliefs or values that are acting as barriers. You must seek to understand the barriers or values that are potentially going to stall or challenge the momentum. This is not a negative but a reality in any improvement process that involves people. Harness the beliefs or values to support the improvement. Set the pace based on understanding rather than deadlines.
- ✓ The Meerkat Effect will play a significant role in building their momentum, having been involved and exposed to the successes of the other teams.

CHAPTER 9

Measured

Figure 9: The SKIM Model: Measured

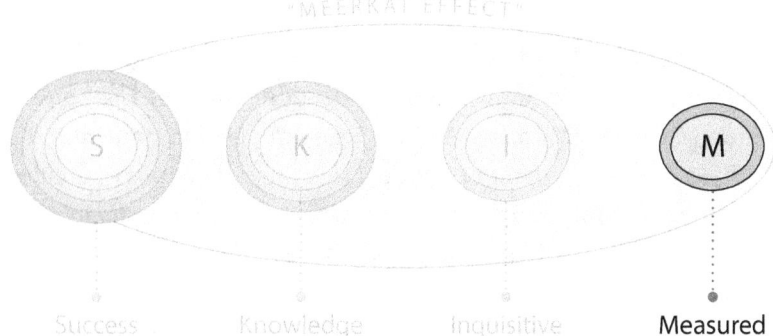

A person who is measured in their thinking and responses is typically described as someone who is cautious, deliberate, thoughtful and calculated in their approach. Such staff can present in many varied ways, including calm and composed while analysing and assessing their thoughts. They can be outwardly confident and critical based on an individual sense of understanding or an approach that can be represented as conflicting where they may dispute arguments as to why they need to improve their understanding of "normal". A measured person would generally avoid impulsiveness and prioritise accuracy, precision and considered judgement, although, I have found at times this perceived "accuracy, precision and considered judgement" can be heavily biased towards the individual and the daunting reality that this improvement agenda might have an adverse impact on their world. Measured Team members may also look to gain the support of their colleagues to build a little more strength towards their perspective (right or wrong). As a leader, these are the team members that can often take a significant amount of your energy and time; however, they can often present with a determination that means we neither move nor improve at any reasonable rate.

In my early leadership days, I spent countless hours and excessive amounts of energy and brain space attempting to motivate and lead the Measured Team from the outset of an implementation or improvement process, and in reflection it was not time well directed. That is in no way a reflection of the staff members that have the default position of being a member of the Measured Team. That reflects my leadership and how I chose to look at the situation. Hargreaves and Fullan, in their book *Professional Capital*, contend that "if you want to get a return, you need to make an investment" (2012, p. 36). It sounds contradictory to what I discussed above about my experience with the Measured Team members. However, I agree with their statement; my contradiction was that I wasn't directing the right energy or motivation to engage this team. As a leader, I struggled to understand their approach, as it was so different to mine. I saw their questions or challenges as a tactic to recruit more supporters or to undermine my leadership status. I had a negative view of their "calculated approach". Hargreaves and Fullan (2012) go on to argue that should a teacher have a different perspective or view to ours, our strategy should never be to argue or be more persuasive with our point of view. Instead, we should take the time to fully understand their point of view, without assumptions and with genuine curiosity.

Arguably, leaders often focus their efforts on the two ends of the continuum:

1. The staff who are enthusiastic and engage in the improvement strategy quickly and eagerly. This is great for our confidence as leaders, as well as giving us the feeling of progress. This is not a negative focus area and does gain a level of momentum towards the improvement agenda. The reality is, even with little energy invested in this enthusiastic group of staff, we are likely to get their support and our time expenditure often doesn't have to be substantial.

2. The other natural space to focus on is the late or slow to adopt – the staff who are adding the challenge to our process. This is often because we want to minimise their potential or perceived negative impact on others. We know that if we can get one of the harder-to-move staff on board, we will have a real sense of achievement and have a level of confidence that we will gain more support and momentum across the school. We also are aware that these staff will take longer to adopt the strategy, so we invest early to give time and spread energy over a longer period of implementation.

These strategies are neither right nor wrong; they are a model of leadership that I have worked within, although I have found this to be less effective in terms of overall momentum and significantly more draining on my leadership teams' energy. The SKIM Model is designed to support a structured, purposeful approach to leading all team members, importantly giving you permission to invest your energy into where you will get the greatest amount of traction in the shortest amount of time. Remember though, we are not letting any staff members off the improvement hook. As we enter the Measured Team approach, they are now only the few remaining staff that need the support and time to jump on board.

You have led with the support of the Success, Knowledge and Inquisitive Teams, the research and evidence of improvement is now clear, and staff can confidently articulate the destination. You haven't invested direct energy into the Measured Team; you have incidentally led them in your staff professional learning, answering and considering their questioning of either the process or the improvement itself. What we cannot forget is that it is not the responsibility of the employee to manage change. Our expectation of our staff should be to simply do their best and consciously seek to improve what we did today so that we are better tomorrow. It is the leader's responsibility to manage change and lead our staff to the point of commitment and advocacy towards the change and improvement agendas.

Dinham (2011) suggests it is unrealistic to think that change will not attract a level of conflict. What we sometimes forget is that it is completely in the hands of everyone as to how they respond or react to any actual or perceived conflict as it arises. As the leader of any group of people, you must consider how you enter any situation with any staff member you are leading.

Do you enter a dialogue with an open curious mind, or do you engage in a monologue and defend the hill you have chosen to stand on? The way you choose to approach the situation or conversation will determine how your staff members respond to you. As Kouzes and Posner (2012) explain in their book *The Leadership Challenge*, great leaders don't simply speak for themselves; they have a responsibility to speak for their teams and their organisations. These leaders appreciate and understand the values of those they are leading and have a way of affirming those staff members and their vision. These leaders "forge unity"; they do not expect it or try to force it. They provide reasons for their teams to care and want to engage, rather than simply feeling that they must follow orders.

I need the Measured Team in my staff room

The Measured Team is a significant piece of the puzzle in every staff room, particularly when we are focusing on leading improvement. The Measured Team make me a better leader and often challenge me and ensure I am more reflective than the other teams in the SKIM Model. Due to their analytic, critical and deliberate approach to new or existing improvement strategies, you can choose to see this technique as opposition or conflict. Or you can choose to reframe your perception and harness their analysis of your leadership process or improvement strategy to reflect, adapt and ultimately make what you do as a leader even better. In the book *Imperfect Leadership*, Munby explains that "leadership is also about an attitude of mind. Feeling good is a skill. You can control it. It is possible to approach difficult situations with joy, provided you are clear about your values and the processes you are going to use. As leaders, we need to walk into the wind, not run away from it" (2019, p. 179).

What a great analogy for leadership – "walking into the wind" – and there is no shortage of windy days! More importantly, as leaders we have a choice about our own attitude, disposition and how we feel about a situation or a challenge. It is an impressive leadership superpower if you know how to activate your "feeling good" and "joy" when they are most needed. I am the first to admit that when I am in cognitive overload and feeling at full capacity, I lose some of my ability to activate that leadership superpower, but it is my responsibility to be extra vigilant and self-aware and know how to get back into a positive frame of mind. With your staff, it comes back to knowing their default positions and behaviours and the professional relationships that you have established around a strong improvement culture.

Throughout all the stages of the SKIM Model, your Measured Team may present themselves in various ways (challenging, withdrawn, analytic, etc.), during the different forums of professional learning or implementation of the improvement strategies. However, because you are very familiar with your team, you can anticipate the possible, probable or potential questions or behaviours that might come your way. This anticipation, considered with positive intent, will boost your leadership capacity and strategy before you walk into the staff room. The key is not to simply anticipate; it is to act. Your actions could look different, depending on your expectations. Having an awareness and preparedness will ensure you do a little more research, a little more analysis, a little more comparison, a little more celebration, a little deeper learning, and a little more collaboration. The purpose is not to be more convincing or persuasive, it is to be more confident, have more clarity, and be prepared to stick to the course with diligence.

The Measured Team will unintentionally be developing your leadership capacity through their approach to improvement. This is simply turning a perceived challenge into an actual opportunity. Defour and Fullan (2013) suggest that determined leaders anticipate disapproval and welcome the opposition rather than criticise. They also argue that these types of leaders don't get discouraged if things do not go as planned; they do not redirect attention because there is something new and exciting to pursue. Finally, they display determination and resilience and ensure they are focused on the set goals and priorities (2013, p. 77). The Measured Team, although they are only the few remaining staff, can offer different and maybe unforeseen perspectives. What a great opportunity to lead with an inclusive and diverse approach!

The alternative is a much gloomier outcome, and one that will take more energy in the longer term than accepting the differences in our teams and adjusting our leadership to support and develop the capacity of each individual member. The risk is a response that all senior leaders (young and old) have most likely come across at some point in their leadership career:

- "I don't agree with this."
- "We have done this before, and it did not work."

- "I haven't been consulted or considered in this decision."
- "This is simply favouring the leadership team."
- "This is going to make my job harder, not easier."
- "I am being manipulated."
- "I will not cooperate."
- "I am going to make this as hard as possible."

I do need to highlight that at no point through the SKIM Model is poor behaviour or unprofessional behaviour acceptable. I will address this in Chapter 12. In every organisation there is a process for poor behaviour and not meeting the expectations of your profession. The SKIM Model is a framework for leading improvement; nevertheless, we will discuss later what to do if it doesn't work.

Now what? So what?

The Measured Team, like all teams, are highly varied in personality, skill, knowledge, capacity, and personal and professional experience. We are leading people, and the unpredictable part of that is that people do not respond according to set criteria. There are many factors and variables that will impact a person's common or uncommon response to any situation. I know how I respond when I am exhausted, so I start to monitor my behaviour or responses. This is followed by a personal intervention, implementing a self-management strategy or two, and I am back on track. For me, that might be going for a walk through classrooms, getting some fresh air, or completing a trivial task to reset. And like all humans, sometimes it gets me before I realise, and I must have a bigger reset. Not all adult learners have this self-awareness, and for the individual or the people around them, it can become normalised behaviour – for example, "It looks like Steve is having one of those days again…" Or you may have had a leader where you wait to see how they enter a space, or the office, before you decide if today is a good day to ask that question. I have had that exact scenario, a daily assessment of what type of leader will walk through the door today. Again, because of this experience, I have worked hard on being a predictable and consistent human leader. We all still have bad days, but I aim for them to be few and far between.

The Measured Team can often have the perception of the unpredictable response, or the predictable response, but not one that we are looking forward to. Have you asked yourself, "Why is this? Why is this staff member's first response negative/defensive/withdrawn etc.?" Until we uncover this, we cannot move beyond normalising this behaviour. This reminds me of an area I was leading for improvement. I had worked through the SKIM Model and was starting to focus additional attention on my Measured Team. We had begun work on digitising our staff curriculum planners. Many of the staff had taken on this task naturally and had led the way through the process. We had all our staff now starting to learn how to use a shared drive with planners online for our teams to access. When we engaged in the improvement process, some of our staff were still completing their planning in a hard-copy (pen and paper) diary. The SKIM Model was successful; all bar one of the staff had shifted online, and although confidence was not high for some, they were giving the improvement process a genuine attempt and getting better by the day.

One staff member, who was an individual we had identified as part of the Measured Team, was struggling with the transition. There were several staff meetings where we discussed the improvement and sought feedback. Initially this staff member was providing feedback – they could not see the point or need for this change. However, as their view became the least favoured in the staff team, they began to avoid the discussions. Our leadership team started to review planners to understand what was working and what was not for the next evolution of the improvement strategy, and we noticed that this staff member had not yet implemented their planner, even at a compliant level. It was time to meet with the staff member to discuss the implementation process. Most importantly, I intended to enter the discussion with a focus on being "curious not furious". I needed to understand the obstacles, the beliefs and values of this staff member, before I could lead them in any direction. It is important to recognise that understanding a staff member's point of view does not mean you have to agree with it, but it allows you to empathise and connect on a mutual understanding. It then empowers you, as leader, to make decisions that will support in moving or minimising the obstacles that are preventing progress.

Defour and Fullan (2013), in their book *Cultures Built to Last*, argue that leaders of all levels promote increased opportunity for others to have success, then they address three key issues:

1. What are the obstacles that are impeding progress?
2. What supports and resources can we provide to improve progress?

3. How can we identify and celebrate progress to increase the opportunity for momentum and individual and organisation confidence?

It was through a curious conversation that we were able to establish where some barriers lay. However, these were not easily obtained from the staff member, and I had to infer and paraphrase throughout our conversation to ensure we both had a good understanding of the situation. The first and most evident obstacle was that they felt completely out of their depth with technology. They could not visualise what the new platform would look like for them; they felt they would not be able to master it or have success. This was based heavily on their past experience with other platforms and programs they had used unsuccessfully. It also highlighted that previously, particularly with technology implementation, they felt they had not had enough support to build their capacity to be successful. The second obstacle was that the time required to learn the skill would potentially have left them behind on their planner, so they felt that their workload and stress levels would increase, and on top of having to learn new skills they would be required to catch up.

Now, I can understand (I do not have to agree) and empathise with this staff member. The most beneficial part of that conversation was that I had a platform on which I could now offer differentiated support. I teamed this staff member up with one of my leaders who had a higher level of expertise and skill with the shared platform, building the planner with them in a very similar learning process to that used in our classrooms – the "gradual release of responsibility" (Fisher & Frey, 2013) – with an adult learner twist. This did not (and will not) mean smooth sailing from here on in; the improvement process is one with many twists and turns, very few of which do not present with new and exciting opportunities to be a learner of learning and a learner of leading.

Man's best friend

I will acknowledge that I too can become a member of the Measured Team. It is not my default, but we all have the capacity to move along the continuum, depending on the topic and how that aligns with our own values and beliefs. This topic I am going to share slowly eats away at me, and although I have good self-control and self-regulation, it does not stop my regular moan about why my beliefs are correct and why others do not demonstrate an understanding of "the right way" of doing things. As a young boy, about five or six years old, my family got a beautiful little puppy – a miniature sheltie collie we called Goldie after my mother's first dog as a child. I remember fondly taking her to her puppy training class, and then to the Advanced Dog School. I cannot recall the instructor's name, but I do recall she was an elderly lady who was very firm with her instructions: "NO, you do not do it like that" or "That is NOT how you hold the lead". I remember having an element of fear each time we went to class on a Saturday morning, but I loved seeing our little Goldie improve her obedience. One of the key skills that must have been drilled into my long-term memory was the importance of always walking your dog on your left-hand side. I recall several of the reasons that still to this day make perfect sense to me:

1. Safety of your dog – In Australia it is a general rule that we walk on the left-hand side of the path (same as our road rules). If the dog owner is walking on the left and they are walking their dog on the left means:
   a. Your dog is walking on the outside of the path, so you can move to the edge and your dog will walk on the grass if needed to move away from oncoming danger or other people/dogs.
   b. Your dog will not be forced to interact with other dogs if you do not want it to, as the two owners will be in between the dogs, with both dogs walking on the owner's left as you pass.
   c. Your dog will not be wandering in the middle of the path, allowing others using the path to pass without having to manoeuvre around your dog.
2. Many dog handlers train their dogs to walk on the left, so they have their right hand free for equipment as needed, opening gates, etc.
3. When riding a horse was the normal form of transport, you mounted the horse on the left, so your dog stayed in vision if it also stayed on the left.
4. I could keep listing many more persuasive arguments from experience, but I will stop there.

Now, it sounds like I am trying to convince you. To be honest, I am a little, and if I convince one person to walk their dog on the left, then I will feel successful. I run three or four times a week around a river near my house.

It is a popular track for runners, riders, kids and dog walkers. Can I highlight that I am an avid dog lover and have a beautiful dog named Lottie, who is also a trained therapy dog and often comes to work with me in this therapy role? She is a border collie and often comes with me on my runs. Now, here is my sticking point: I run on the left with my dog on my left; however, I often have to zigzag, run on the grass or dirt, or move off the path, due to other people's dogs being walked on the right and therefore being in the middle of the path. In fact, sometimes there will be multiple people with multiple dogs and the humans have to move off the path because their dogs are taking up most of the space. I am sure you can hear the frustrated tone in my writing.

My values and beliefs around this simple task of respectfully walking your dog in public are embedded. They are a part of what I believe is responsible and respectful dog walking. However, I acknowledge that these are MY beliefs and values, and I am sure there are many others who have differing points of view on this topic. I have built this narrative over almost 35 years, so if someone simply says to me that there are other options that form a better outcome for all, it will not land constructively for me. I will need more than words to change my perspective. I will need more than the perspective of another person who may not have completed the same "advanced dog training" as I did with my Goldie. The point is, if we cannot understand the values and beliefs of others, and use this as the starting point for improvement, we will find ourselves in a space where unconstructive rebuttal and conflict thrive. As an experienced leader, I can admit that maybe my view is not the consensus of all. Nonetheless, I feel the frustration build. The more tired or cognitively overloaded I am, the more it hits me. Some of your staff who have the default position of the Measured Team may not always have the capacity to see the topic or focus area from another's viewpoint. As the leader, it is our responsibility to firstly seek to understand, then find a way to lead staff members forward and give them a slightly different or adjusted perspective.

Discussion

Now that you are into the final stages of the SKIM Model, you will have the majority of staff on the "improvement bus". As I have articulated, the SKIM Model is not about letting any of our team off the hook. Part of the professional obligations in almost every organisation is improvement; we have established that this is an inevitable part of our professional lives. The Measured Team have had access to the learning, the Meerkat Effect celebrations, consultation and evidence. It is now time for this team to join the majority. As we have discussed, the initial steps are based on compliance rather than commitment. This may have already become present during the Inquisitive Team's approach. As with all leadership of staff, this may not come naturally or immediately; however, it is important that we establish a clear pathway for the members to see the line of sight to the destination. By this stage many, if not all, of the obstacles have been identified, and things have been put in place to minimise or remove these.

So, I am sure you are wondering, what about the one or two staff members who still are not budging or seem to be "digging in their heels"? I will address this more in Chapter 12; however, there is truth in the old adage "You can lead a horse to water…" In every step of any leadership model, or any other process for that matter, there is choice. With every choice there is a reasonable outcome. The SKIM Model is not a tool to manage staff performance or determine accountability or organisation expectation processes. There are formalised procedures for that in almost every organisation. The SKIM Model is a framework to build momentum through intentional and differentiated leadership, allowing you to lead with purpose; more importantly, to enjoy leading the varied individuals within your organisation.

Leadership reflection task

What situation or activity would place you in the Measured Team if there was suggested change or improvement?

- ☐ What values or beliefs do you hold that are possible barriers or challenges that could make an improvement process in your identified area difficult?
- ☐ How could this be perceived by the leader of the change?
- ☐ Is there a situation that you can reflect on in your leadership where you have encountered this? How did you handle the situation? What could/would you do differently next time?

Measured Team – Quick take-aways

✓ The Measured Team is often portrayed unfairly as "the negative staff" or referred to as "laggards" (Rogers, 1962). They can be perceived as the frustrating staff that challenge leaders with personal agendas.

✓ They are an essential part of the improvement process. This team is a part of almost every organisation; not only should we accept that as the reality of leading, but we should also embrace the challenge and be curious about their position in any improvement process.

✓ This team force us to be a more informed leader. We know that the Measured Team will be analysing our professional or adult learning, finding holes in the data or evidence, asking challenging questions, and being confident in their rebuttal of the strategy. In knowing this, we ensure that we prepare more, understand more, research more, and walk into a room with more knowledge and confidence in the improvement strategy so that we are prepared for and welcome robust discussions around the improvement process.

✓ They are only a small percentage; however, they often take a significant amount of our energy early in an improvement process. Do not move the spotlight to the Measured Team until it is their turn to engage.

✓ Understand their beliefs and values before leading. Before you can fully engage this team in the improvement process, you must understand their stance or position and why or what are the beliefs and values that are enabling their actions. Until you understand, you may be employing the least effective strategies to support these members to adjust their values and beliefs and jump on board the improvement process.

CHAPTER 10

The Meerkat Effect

Figure 10: The SKIM Model: The "Meerkat Effect"

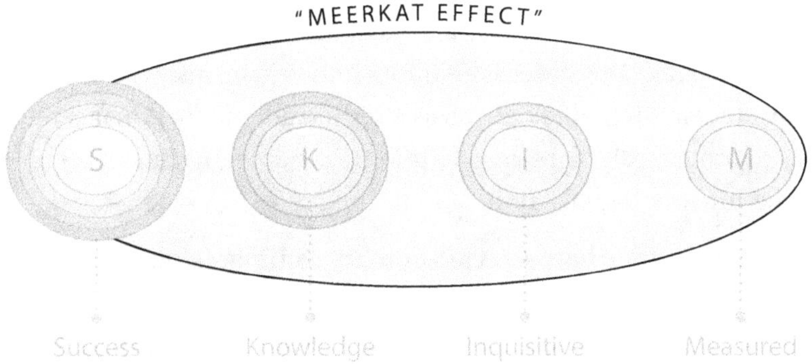

"MEERKAT EFFECT"

S — Success
K — Knowledge
I — Inquisitive
M — Measured

In the early 2000s, Meerkats stole the spotlight with a docuseries that narrated their lives, adventures, triumphs and dynasties. I recall the territorial mobs battling over lands and love, but mostly I remember the iconic stance of the meerkat, on top of their burrow, on the lookout. This was a curious yet cautious pose, at the top of their mounds, looking for dangers, while portraying a comical expressive pose of FOMO (Fear of Missing Out).

"Hey what's going on over there?" "Who is that?" "What are they up to?" "That looks fun, can I play?"

This curious and investigative image of the meerkat is what has driven the analogy and purpose of the "Meerkat Effect" in the SKIM Model. This visual image provides the platform for a process that is embedded in the entirety of the SKIM Model. Effective leadership of the Meerkat Effect will generate more than curiosity and is a platform for more than celebrations of small or big wins in the improvement process. We must be purposeful in its implementation, have a clear method in which we are building the momentum, confidence and capacity of the staff we are leading.

A trap can be that we lead with only positive celebrations of the implementation of the improvement agenda. However, we cannot rely on positive exposure of small wins and hope that this will lead to the development of our teams. Dinham (2011) suggests that it is a gamble to focus purely on the "contagious effect" of committed staff demonstrating success, or as it is titled in the SKIM Model, the Meerkat Effect. Dinham (2011) believes that this might engage some of the hesitant or negative staff members but that it will not engage all. I agree with this proposition. If we rely purely on the Meerkat Effect as a vehicle only for celebrations or to gain commitment to the improvement strategy, we will be left with a number of compliant or disconnected staff. This process – although the visual imagery of a meerkat standing at their post could be seen as cute and adorable – is in fact required to be a rigorous, well-planned, intentional process to achieve the desired outcomes for your organisation.

From the moment you have selected the best skimming stone (improvement agenda), the Meerkat Effect begins to take shape. Every member of your organisation who will be involved or impacted by the improvement process must be involved from the introduction of the "why?" or the evidence, goals or targets that led you and your leadership team to select that particular stone. Before you start to engage the Success Team in the implementation, they, like the rest of the SKIM Model, need exposure, and a level of understanding must be communicated and discussed. It is at this point that the Meerkat Effect becomes the vessel for development of the improvement vision and initial direction. Everyone must be involved in this process in a planned ongoing manner.

Kouzes and Posner (2012), in their book *The Leadership Challenge*, argue that visions that are only seen, and I would argue constructed, by leaders are inadequate and have an incredibly low success rate in creating organisational movement. We discussed the selection of the Success Team in Chapter 6 as being a process of selecting the "right" team, not the "easy" team. For your Success Team to start the improvement process on the right foot, they must have a collective level of understanding of what it is that the organisation is leading. For the Success Team to be successful and start the momentum moving in the desired direction, these early consultative and collaborative discussions must ensure that the initial SKIM team you select will be the right team who will have the greatest influence on the positive energy of the improvement process, rather than the easy team, who are sometimes putting their hands up, yelling out "Lead me – I am not sure what it is, but I will do it!" I know I have also said that if a staff member wants to learn, I will not say no; we can also acknowledge that some of those initial staff will engage in the process with little additional attention from leadership. So let them, while ensuring you follow the rigorous Success Team selection process that will ensure you have a robust, broad and influential team to begin the improvement progression.

The Meerkat Effect is a process that is reliant on leadership that has unconditional positive intent towards the people they lead. They passionately advocate for their teams and individuals, believing that each member can make a positive difference to their organisation and culture. Importantly, they invest time in generating excitement about the possibilities and potential that the future holds. They must be able to communicate clearly and build trust and clarity around how individual and collective values can have a positive impact on the organisation's future. Thus, the leader's responsibility, as part of the Meerkat Effect, is to generate an environment that will facilitate a collective and aligned vision of what the possibilities are when we move as a united team.

If it is not "cute", what is it?

We have established that people thrive with a level of challenge. We have also discussed how this challenge needs to be differentiated to support the needs and entry point of every staff member we lead. Kouzes and Posner argue that our staff do their best when they are in a position where they are provided with an opportunity to make change. They go on to advocate that "progress is not made in giant leaps; it is made incrementally. Exemplary leaders move forward in small steps with little victories. They turn adversity into advantage, setbacks into successes. They persevere with grit and determination" (2012). The Meerkat Effect will be positioned for success and positive impact when leaders are transparent in challenge and obstacles, consult, and are open to other views, particularly on minimising or removing obstacles. Leaders also "take a hit" for these obstacles or challenges, knowing that various types of difficulties are simply part of the improvement process, not a reflection of you or your teams. As Marzano et al. (2014) argue, by identifying and acknowledging these problems or obstacles, we can resolve them before they have a significant impact. More importantly, leaders use the Meerkat Effect to acknowledge others. Allowing your teams to take the spotlight and credit for successes makes sure that everyone feels like they are winning in the improvement process.

A great question to ask yourself or your leadership team when you are planning the implementation of the Meerkat Effect process is:

How do I want my teams to feel about the identified improvement agenda when they leave this session?

This remarkably simple question acknowledges the influence you have as a leader when designing sessions, conversations, collaboration or learning that can leave staff feeling confident and inspired or discouraged and disconnected, and can reframe the direction of your learning architecture. What outcome or message do you want your teams to leave with, and how can you design an engaging, confidence-building session to get them there?

The key to leading this outcome is understanding the power of influence within the Meerkat Effect. Influence must be genuine and be led with positive intent. Dellaert and Davydov argue that through influence leaders can "shape the right organisational culture, work collectively with teams on the design and implementation of the strategy to get people aligned to the vision and strategic goals" (2017, p. 11). However, leaders must have clarity around their motivations with influence. A quite simple and possibly unintentional deviation can change influence from a positive motivation and momentum tool within the Meerkat Effect to a power-based process that can be interpreted by staff as manipulation. Influence is heavily based on trusting, professional relationships, clear and transparent goals, and direction on how this improvement will align to personal and organisational values. If these are not established and are not seen as genuine, then power and manipulation can overshadow our team's perception. It might be suspected that there is a hidden agenda that the leader will benefit from; the leader might be seen as trying to take advantage or expose a weakness of an individual or team. They may feel that they are being forced to adhere rather than being led to understand. A leader positioning themselves to be perceived as the lead power player or a manipulator can unravel and fracture an organisation's culture quicker than a parent dropping their child back at school after the summer break.

How do I activate the Meerkat Effect?

When I envisage a meerkat, the visual that pops into my head is a small, furry animal curiously asking, "What's that over there? That looks fun; maybe I will have a closer look." Ideally, this is similar to the response over time of your teams. They can see the magnificent work happening, they start to understand the theory or research, they have been exposed to the evidence of improvement. They see there is minor risk to their values, because they have had input, collaborative and consultative opportunities, to help develop and implement the plan through feedback and adult learning.

We must also acknowledge that the opposite may happen if we are not intentional in our planning. Our staff, particularly our Inquisitive and Measured Teams, may see the improvement as a bigger risk, not understanding the evidence or being unable see how this strategy will have a positive impact. Most importantly, if they have not had the opportunity to provide feedback, collaborate, trial, disagree or provide alternative points of view, then the Meerkat Effect will have a more negative impact: "What is happening over there? That looks dangerous. Let's band together to protect ourselves from this terrifying thing that is occurring."

Amabile and Kramer (2011) explain that if there is anything that will motivate staff or boost positive emotions at a workplace, it is feeling like you are making progress in work you value. The Meerkat Effect is the space where we can lead discussions, put our celebrations on display, allow robust conversations about progress, and put the teams or staff in the spotlight when we have seen improvement, even the smallest amount. The Meerkat

Effect is more than celebrating the wins and successes, although this has a significant impact on our staff disposition towards the improvement. Elmore argues that "the process of cultural change depends fundamentally on modelling the new values and behaviors that you expect to displace existing ones" (2004, p. 11). Therefore, the role of the Meerkat Effect is to focus on modelling the cultural change you are aiming to achieve. The cultural change could be implementing discussions that challenge or contest ideas, which can lead to a healthy discussion about evidence and data comparisons to make sure our decisions are the right ones.

Without limiting the possibilities of a collaborative discussion that could surface a pathway or discussion you have not encountered or foreseen, consider the following examples of possible Meerkat Effect outcomes:

1. Celebrations and acknowledgements of small wins and staff success.
2. Presentations of progress by the SKIM teams as they gain momentum.
3. Mentoring or peer observations.
4. Research or evidence-based adult learning.
5. Exposure to the challenges of implementation and discussion about how to resolve obstacles.
6. Collaborative planning, discussions or brainstorming.
7. Developing, communicating and implementing the improvement vision.
8. Continual reference back to the vision and purpose of the improvement strategy.
9. Ongoing acknowledgement of the team's effort.
10. Ongoing reference to evidence as it evolves or changes with the review of and reflection on the improvement strategy.

As you activate your Meerkat Effect, the most effective platform is your professional learning sessions where everyone is involved and has a voice. Cheliotes and Reilly propose that "a principal may delineate a multi-step action plan for school improvement, but sustained growth and change are not likely to occur unless all constituencies of the school accept the plan as their own and feel supported as they implement new initiatives" (2010, p. 2). The Meerkat Effect is the platform for voice, debate, support and acceptance. Without this space, and without an intentional leadership framework such as the SKIM Model, there is an increased chance that you will be investing excessive energy with little gain.

Munro and Campbell, in their article *Coaching as a Way of Leading*, suggest that "the people centered way of leading enhances relational trust, empowers others, and enhances wellbeing through more agency-enabling conversations that support progress" (2022, p. 32). What a list of people-focused attributes! Few leaders would not want their teams to walk away from an adult learning session feeling empowered, with greater levels of trust and agency and an increase sense of personal or cultural wellbeing. The Meerkat Effect is the vehicle to support the development of these personal and team characteristics. We know that if a leader simply wants staff to agree with the idea or proposed improvement agenda or direction, then they are not overly concerned or genuine about the thoughts of the staff member. An activated Meerkat Effect is not a "top-down" leadership model. It enables voice and agency among your staff. It encourages discussion and ownership over the vision and direction. The momentum is generated from a sense of achievement and progress, through the acknowledgement and recognition of the success of teams and individuals. Leadership generates the energy, modelling enthusiasm and anticipation of the positive outcomes. The Meerkat Effect gives the individuals or teams that the change is going to impact the opportunity to have input into how it will be managed and at what pace it will be implemented. If our team is not on board, the improvement strategy will not have sustained success.

Mark the meerkat

Mathematics was my team's next priority of focus linked to our overarching goals and targets. One of the first identified areas of improvement – our selected skimming stone – was the consistent development and use of a yearly curriculum overview, or essential learnings. To say we did not have a form of overview is incorrect. Every one of our staff used a version that they had acquired over years of teaching and learning and had it on rotation. Some were using a variety they had found at the beginning of a mathematics or numeracy resource book, some adapted planning from the previous year to follow a similar topic delivery over the following year. Many had an overview that had evolved in many forms and been handed down from a team member or mentor they believed was reliable and a good teacher of the subject. None of these approaches are wrong, and all would have merit in the process or way they deliver the curriculum.

The challenge with this style of implementation, though it is not an uncommon method of adaption and application, is that we end up with different and inconsistent learning experiences depending on the classroom and teacher or team that is planning mathematics. It also means we do not have a "Guaranteed and Viable Curriculum" (Marzano et al., 2014, p. 57). Marzano et al. suggest that "Guaranteed" implies that all teachers are aware of the content and are teaching that content, while "Viable" suggests that the content is accessible and teachable (2014, p. 57). I argue – and maybe it is trivial – that we first need to have a viable curriculum, one that is robust, actionable, consistently understood and applied, with the structures and resources to support the implementation. Only then can we guarantee our curriculum's impact through assessment and improvement of teaching and learning outcomes.

My leadership team had established the initial pathway using the Meerkat Effect, building the vision and understanding of the overarching mathematics goals and targets with our whole team, entering the professional learning session with an open-minded approach to build "the why" with the whole team. We had a "pencilled" plan of attack to gain the interest in and understanding of the planned improvement outcome and a proposed summary of how we might get there, and who we believed would potentially make up the Success Team to have the greatest impact and build the early momentum. Please note that I said "pencilled plan", "how we might get there" and "potentially make up the Success Team". These words are very intentional. With genuine curiosity, we know our staff may support our leadership to find a different and better path to the outcome. We need to have a plan; our teams want to know we have a plan. But we need to have the flexibility to adapt and pivot if a different, better or more rigorous pathway presents itself.

In the first professional learning session, we started with the goals, targets, proposed outcomes, and the possible improvement process. We entered a discussion with staff to initially get a genuine idea of where everyone was at. We started with a simple prompt: "What do you use to plan mathematics?" We were clear that there is no right or wrong; there is simply a here and now. This is what we currently do, and this is how we do it. Until we have established a starting point, we cannot value add, improve or adapt. This part of any improvement process is built through a genuine consultative, collaborative and curious approach. Staff will know if there is a "hidden agenda".

We collated the discussion and moved to our second stage of building the vision and momentum: "What does the research say?" Not long into the adult learning session, the session leader asked, "How can we offer our students a more consistent experience in mathematics at every level, every day?" Mark, known for being a confident, passionate and at times blunt staff member, simply said, "My planner is great. I teach everything I need to, and my kids love what I teach." The session leader had several options in responding to Mark. He could have rebutted Mark's comment, because he had not yet shared the whole school data and trends that did not support Mark's comment that "I teach everything I need to". He could have agreed that Mark's kids love mathematics, but also pointed out that Mark's planner still did not reflect the curriculum as a whole. However, before "returning serve", the session leader reflected: "What do I want to achieve from this adult learning session? How do I want my staff feeling when they leave? What would I achieve from giving Mark a few evidence-based truths at this early stage of the SKIM Model?" The answer is that we would have achieved little, and in fact it would have set Mark a long way back from engaging and most likely put a few other staff members off as collateral damage.

The leader who was running the session answered perfectly: "Thank you, Mark, your kids do love maths. Let us all get an understanding of what the research says about consistency in our approach, and could I catch you later to get a copy of your overview to help me understand how you plan maths for your students?" Mark nodded, and having been acknowledged, participated in the remainder of the session. Before my leader caught up with Mark, we had a pre-discussion about what outcome we wanted from the discussion. We produced three simple questions:

1. Why did Mark value his maths overview?
2. How did he use it?
3. What was the basis or theory behind his overview?

The maths overview that Mark had been using was from an extremely popular brand of maths resource books, I would guess that several more editions had been published after the one that was being referenced. Not only did it have a week-by-week planner, but it also had links to a student resource activity book and lesson plans. Mark was not a teacher who often used worksheets as his go-to for teaching and tended to use the idea of the lesson from the resource to make it more creative and engaging for the students. Mark had been using this resource for years; it had been introduced to him by a teacher he respected, many years earlier. Mark maintained that it covered the essential curriculum in mathematics and that the structures it provided supported his planning and ensured that all areas of the curriculum were covered, although the leader who was supporting the conversations advised me that it seemed to be more of a tick-and-move-on process than an overview that supported differentiated instruction. However, whether we agreed with this or not, these were Mark's beliefs. Saying that his beliefs were wrong or not founded in research or evidence would not have resulted in a positive outcome for Mark or the improvement process that was to follow. What we were aiming to do was get a clear understanding of Mark's point of view, his perception of the improvement agenda, so that as a leadership team we could differentiate what we offered Mark to ensure we were leading him rather than forcing or directing him to the destination. The individuals who would be most impacted by a negative outcome in this situation in the long run were Mark's students.

The first step was to clearly communicate that we were not asking Mark to change his model, at that point in time. Mark's default position was as a Measured Team member; we were not going to invest the extra time into Mark's engagement, yet. We were, however, going to harness the opportunities in the Meerkat Effect to ensure that when we got to the Measured Team, Mark was ready to go. We asked Mark, and a selected handful of other staff members, to list what it was about their current overview that they valued. We also asked what the challenges were that they had come across. Over the next few sessions, we put on the table all the different overviews that were being used or accessed. We also added some overviews from schools that were high performing in mathematics as examples. Mark and his fellow selected staff members did not present their overview so that they could argue why it was the best one; they presented the points that they had developed about what they valued in the documents they used and what challenges they found. We gave Mark a voice, so that he could articulate his values in a way that focused on what helps in teaching mathematics and what some of the obstacles are. This discussion was used as a platform to then produce a list of things that support teaching and learning in an overview. We linked the information to the initial research from our adult learning sessions. We deconstructed the high-performing school's overviews and rebuilt, referring to our set of criteria.

Throughout this process, Mark was not only involved in the work, he was fully engaged. He had the opportunity to have a voice, and his voice was not rebutted, it was refined to align with our purpose and direction. By the time we got to our Inquisitive Team, Mark's enthusiasm and eagerness for the reconstructed overview encouraged our leaders to move him from his potential default position in the Measured Team to the Inquisitive Team. He had started to trial the change independently, without communicating this to our leaders. He was "dipping his toes in" to check the temperature and realised that the change was an improvement and still supported what he valued. It did not invalidate his beliefs or voice. As an organisation, we had achieved a significant outcome with Mark, but given that Mark was only one of the team members, our work was not complete.

Discussion

The Meerkat Effect is not a one-off session. We don't just move on to our next learning opportunity and assume that, because we got a good vibe in the collaboration with our teams, we now have everyone on board. Cheliotes and Reilly (2010) claim that sometimes conversations are not productive because we have not fully considered or gathered enough information about the other's perspective. We can fail to see the signs, both verbal and non-verbal, of disengagement or that a staff member needs support. Instead, we may have a predetermined pathway of action and process to get to the outcome. The Meerkat Effect is an ongoing, consistent and intentional opportunity to gain, build and sustain momentum. The Meerkat Effect will run the entirety of your improvement agenda and will continue to evolve and reappear as you revisit existing opportunities if the momentum begins to slow or deviate within your organisation. "Problem prevention is an excellent reason to constantly monitor critical factors and address errors immediately. However, it is not the only reason to monitor performance. Tracking performance and using quick data allows school leaders to celebrate successes" (Marzano et al., 2014. p. 11). We discussed the importance of using the Meerkat Effect to highlight successes; however, we also acknowledge that success comes from teams and individuals solving challenging problems or overcoming identified difficulties. The environment needs to be both challenging and celebratory, robust, and reflective, consultative and collaborative. It is a complex balance; however, remember that improvement is not a race, although at times it seems like it is, or you may have little control of the tempo due to external pressures. As a leader of your organisation, you are in charge of the pace, so take the time you need to ensure you are getting the greatest impact from the Meerkat Effect.

Leadership reflection task

- ☐ How do you celebrate staff effort and achievement?
- ☐ Do all staff get a taste of team or individual celebration?

Consider a recent conversation, team discussion or professional learning session that did not go as planned:

- ☐ How do you think your team was left feeling at the completion of the session/conversation?
- ☐ Why do you perceive they were left feeling that way?
- ☐ What was the intended feeling you wanted from the session?
- ☐ How might you use the Meerkat Effect to achieve a different response in the future?

The Meerkat Effect – Quick take-aways

- ✓ This provides an active positive exposure to all staff in an ongoing manner – formal and informal (professional learning, collaborative planning, staff conversations, learning space exposure, colleague presentations) opportunities to celebrate and expose staff to the improvement focus area.
- ✓ Like a meerkat observing from the safety of their burrow, your SKIM teams will be looking for success and danger or risk before engaging. It is essential that we are not "sugar coating" the

improvement process; that we are transparent and collaborative about the challenges, the failures, and the successes; and that as a whole staff we are working together to problem-solve or celebrate.

- ✓ All staff need to be celebrated and acknowledged for any small or large improvement opportunity. Celebration could also look like a challenging question that is celebrated because it has highlighted a potential barrier.
- ✓ The SKIM teams lead the Meerkat Effect through celebrating success and evidence of improvement. The people implementing the improvement process and strategy must also be the ones leading the discussions. The leader facilitates, supports and leads with intentional process and direction.
- ✓ Improvement momentum will be built or paused through the implementation of the Meerkat Effect. Every opportunity should be taken to expose staff to the potential of implementing the improvement strategy successfully.
- ✓ Persuading/convincing staff to engage in improvement is not a Meerkat Effect strategy. If you find yourself trying to persuade staff, step back and review the vision and purpose of the improvement strategy. If you have selected the right stone, positive intentional and planned leadership will get you the momentum rather than a persuasive approach.

PART 3
Other considerations

CHAPTER 11
Language is important

Several years ago, a friend of mine, Trav, approached me explaining that he and some of his colleagues were planning on entering a rowing team in the annual "Head of the River" event in the corporate section. He then proceeded to ask if I would be interested in joining the team. I was surprised and chuffed that I had been asked. I replied, "I would love to, Trav, but unfortunately I have never rowed before." With a little smirk, he responded, "We were actually hoping you would be the cox." I felt a small percentage of embarrassment and disappointment, but a large percentage of pride that I was the lightest, most coordinated small person they knew.

The team was made up of four rowers, all of whom had rowed through high school and university, and a coxswain (cox), me. The cox was responsible for steering the boat and coordinating the power and rhythm of the rowers. Not only had I never rowed before; I had also never been a cox; in fact, other than seeing boats on the river and my high school having rowing teams, I had never experienced anything to do with rowing. Our first of four practices was on a Sunday morning, and the team had organised to borrow a boat from a local rowing club. I received a 5-minute introduction to coxing and then headed straight into the water.

The four rowers hadn't rowed together before and were spending some time working out their positions and timings. Really, they were all talking a foreign language to me as I sat at the back of the shell (the name of the rowing boat). While the rowers' conversation was going on and we were floating in the river, I was looking at the two skinny wires running down the side of my seat. These were for steering; however, they had to be aligned with the rowers' balance and power. It was a lot more complex than I thought. Like all new learning, I was in an unfamiliar position with skills I hadn't yet acquired or even understood at this point. On top of that, I had a team of experienced rowers relying on me in the role of cox. I felt the pressure.

I vividly remember the first 20 minutes or so. The team supported me by steering using the power or released power of their oars. We slowly got to the end of the course, and I could see the team was not able to continue with the support they had been providing me. They had to keep looking over their shoulder to make sure we were heading in the right direction or at least going somewhat straight. I knew that was my responsibility, and that they needed to focus on rowing, so I had to perform my role as cox. We pulled up, looking straight down the river to the finish line. I counted in and off we went, and by "off we went" I mean that we took a sharp right turn and headed straight towards the bank. Initially, in a meek voice, I said, "Hey guys, I think we should stop... um stop... STOP, WE ARE GOING TO CRASH!" And crash we did, into the reeds, with a few frustrated and confused faces and me sitting there bemused that the boys kept rowing when I was clearly yelling "STOP!"

We regrouped, and one of the team members said, "If you want us to stop, you need to yell out 'Easy oar'. That tells us we need to stop." I was now confused; what part of "Stop, we are going to crash" is not clear enough to make people stop rowing? This highlighted the importance of the language we use that is specific to particular environments. "Before the next practice," he said, pulling out his phone, "look at this website that has a list of words that are the language of rowing." It was important that the language I used was clear and accurate. The team understood "Stop, we are going to crash"; however, they were in rowing mode. Their language radar had been switched to the specific and precise language that rowers use. "Easy oar", said once and clearly, signified an action that connected to their long-term memory. The language of rowing is absolutely essential to ensure a common platform in which to communicate. Three practices later, we entered the competition. There were four other teams in the corporate event. Our team clicked. I had the language, they had the technical skills, and we ended up winning by 4–5 boat lengths. From the start to the finish of the race, I yelled every rowing word I could remember in a sequence that the crew understood. The rowers won the race, but the language played an essential role in making sure the entire team understood expectations and decisions and worked in unison. They knew when to go at maximum speed ("Power 10 or 20") and when to pull back ("Settle"). We worked as one cohesive team built around a common and specific language. The team did not need to learn new words or my language. Their cognitive load could focus on effort and teamwork, because the rowing language was clear and triggered specific actions, a process that was already learnt.

The power of words

Munro and Campbell (2022), argue that conversations and leadership go hand in hand. They suggest that, regardless of the policy and structure of any organisation, progress will be inhibited or supported based on how we talk to each other and, just as importantly, what we talk about. The power of language cannot be disputed; we have all encountered misunderstandings, whether personal or professional, where there has been a misinterpretation or misuse of language that has caused confusion or even conflict, only to later discover that the intentions were not what had been thought.

Defour and Fullan have suggested that "consistent and effective communication demands that leaders align their own behavior and the processes of the organisation with its stated goals and priorities" (2013, p. 25). They go on to argue that if leaders are misaligned or inconsistent in language, we get confusion that can undermine the improvement process or a leader's credibility. The language of improvement can build momentum and a consistent understanding of what each of our key terms means and looks like, or our conversations can have an adverse effect where we cannot connect to the variables of the language used and so our communication and conversations will also have high levels of differing understanding and variability. This is supported by Groysberg and Slind (2012) and Walker and Aritz (2014), who discuss how the traditional style of leadership had a heavy focus on the leader themselves – who they are, what they did – and put the spotlight on the leader for achievement in an improvement process. However, they argue that "conversational approaches" focus on the relationships and the collaboration between the leader and those who are being led. Therefore, at the beginning of an improvement process – firstly with the leadership team who will be serving as the facilitators of the improvement agenda, and then with the staff as a whole through the Meerkat Effect – the common, consistent and expected language must be explicitly discussed and intentionally used. I will continue to argue that conversations are the catalyst for momentum in any organisation; however, to have healthy discussions and evidence-based professional debates, we firstly must agree on the language and meaning of what it is we are doing. Referring back to my earlier example, in the language of rowing "Easy oar" means stop, and I am sure we could think of many examples of synonyms that we could throw in there as well. In the rowing space, the language is important and has agreed meaning. I unfortunately was not aware of this language and the value it held prior to crashing.

One of my long-term friends, Xave, has worked as a senior leader in the safety industry over many years and in many large government sectors. One of the key phrases that he has mentioned as being reasonably common is "Hurry up and wait". This is used when there is an emergency or a particular team activation will be required – for example, fire fighters are about to be deployed. The staff in the organisation who are on call or need to travel to the destination of the emergency are often buzzing with anticipation, have a lot of adrenaline pumping, and are wasting significant amounts of energy in eagerness to put their skills into action. The term "Hurry up and wait" signifies the importance of patience and calmness until you can initiate your skills, to ensure that the team are composed and regulate their level of anxiety and pressure prior to performing their roles.

This is like the language used in education – for example, in a teacher's instructional model, the term "explicit teaching". If the teaching team who need to understand the specific language do not have a clear, effective, consistent understanding of what is required of them, the term "explicit teaching" will be up for interpretation and inconsistent implementation. Understanding what "explicit teaching", "Easy oar" or "Hurry up and wait" mean, and then having a set of learnt actions that are required, also has a considerable impact on reducing the team's or individual's cognitive load (discussed in Chapter 5). When language is explicitly linked to actions that are agreed, practised and refined, it means that when that language is used, staff in any organisation don't have to take time to think about the process; they can move to the expected action. The language is moved from their short-term memory into their long-term memory, leaving more space for new learning. The SKIM Model will do that when you are leading improvement. The process becomes learnt, so you can focus on where the biggest impact on improvement lies – with your people.

Language can be inclusive or exclusive

Several years ago, our network was offered a learning opportunity focused on middle leaders in schools (learning specialists, leading teachers). The intention of the professional learning session was positive and meaningful, acknowledging that these particular leaders needed some additional learning opportunities to support their growth as leaders and increase their pathway into more senior leadership. It was an important area for development and one in which there seemed to be an increasing gap in the development of our future school leaders. The network at the time had a unique context. We were a very broad network spanning quite a large geographical distance, with a very diverse range of schools. We had schools of 12 students right up to schools with over 1500 students – small primary schools, large secondary schools, and Prep to Year 12 schools. Over a third of our schools had under 100 students. So, although I acknowledge the importance of the focus on middle leaders, for this network, this excluded many schools, with those under 100 and some slightly above not having the capacity to have any middle leaders. In these schools the principal was in a unique position in that they were both the senior leader and a teacher and often wore every other hat in between. Nevertheless, the professional learning for middle leaders may have been valuable for some of these principals of smaller schools, particularly if they were new to the role, or possibly for some of their teachers who in these smaller schools took on a role equivalent to that of a middle leader, often without being given time out of the learning space. The title "middle leaders" gave a perception that your title gave you membership, rightly or wrongly.

Specific language communicates a specific intention. I have unintentionally done this in my conversations with my teams before. I have had whole staff learning that included my teaching and education support staff where I have stood up at the front and said, "Welcome, teachers..." I have never had a staff member come and say, "You did not welcome the education support staff", because I have often corrected myself and changed it to "educators" or "staff" later on. However, I would completely understand if a staff member felt excluded by an unintended use of exclusive language.

The other important thing to recognise is that the value of language can be undermined, watered down, and lose some of its significance when it is used too much, inappropriately, or interchangeably with other inconsistent language. One term that has seemed to increase in use over the last decade is the word "bullying". Bullying is an extremely serious and endemic issue that can be seen in various forms in industries and organisations worldwide. The increased use of social media has highlighted the hidden effects that bullying can have on people young and old, with a significant amount of research and time being put into supporting programs and initiatives to highlight its effects and educate the public. I am not going to challenge the severity and consequences of bullying and the need to continually address this through education. However, more and more behaviours of concern are now being referred to as bullying. Sometimes it is "I was bullied today" or "My child was bullied yesterday", and in many cases this refers to an incident of being picked on or teased, name calling, a physical altercation, significant behaviours of concern or safety risks. All these behaviours and any others that impact the safety or wellbeing of any person in a school or other organisation are not in any way OK and need to be addressed. These may be bullying type behaviours, or might lead to bullying if continued; however, by referring to all of these behaviours as bullying, I fear we lose the significance of what bullying is and the impact it has on people. Education is the key, but it is also difficult to tackle an emotive response when someone feels that they, their child, a family member, or a friend has had a negative experience due to another person – which is still not OK.

I wish that a clever wordsmith could create new terminology that identifies the different stages of bullying, so that bullying is an overarching term used for negative behaviours that impact others' safety or wellbeing but we also have a term for when these behaviours turn from a bullying type of behaviour into actual bullying. Clarity around what words mean and don't mean can alter the impact of terminology, titles and other words.

There are many words in every organisation that we sometimes refer to in jest as "buzz words" – language that we often hear in conversations about an organisation's trends or theory of practice. I can remember thinking at university: "Pedagogy – I will never use that in a sentence again!" And here I am doing precisely that. However, we can sometimes begin to use purposeful, important language in such a way that it becomes meaningless. More often than not, I get a "gut feeling" if the language that is being used is genuine or a buzz word. Two examples are "consultation" and "feedback", which are too often used carelessly. However, if we want to build our staff's trust and cultural and professional wellbeing, we must seek to use these two very simple words, which have profound meanings, only for a genuine purpose. If we say at the end of emails, "Please let me know if you have any feedback", or if we open a discussion with the promise of consultation, and then we don't actively seek the input and feedback from our teams, these words, like many others, will become undermined and watered down and will lose their significance.

Ratanjee (2021), in the article *Successful Organizational Change Needs a Strong Narrative*, suggests that leaders shape the culture and attitude towards change through building a compelling narrative that can create trust, intrigue and clarity in the improvement process. Our worlds are built around stories; this is how we discuss and make sense of many situations in our personal and professional lives. Think of the number of situations where you have connected to an event or positioned your beliefs due to having a similar story that helped you connect to what something feels, sounds or looks like. Leading improvement is no different; we are connecting our teams to a narrative of improvement where they feel they can understand, feel, connect, recall or sympathise with the story. However, we must have clarity and trust to build staff engagement, so your story must be non-fiction and based around a common language and understanding of what we are talking about. If people are reading your improvement story and must infer meaning instead of having a literal understanding, then we cannot confidently say that our teams will infer the same outcome.

A rural school I was leading was on a septic system due to our location. The system was installed a long, long time ago and was at the bottom of the school block. Over time, the school had been redeveloped, and the slope of the land meant that the septic was now where all our stormwater also flowed.

Any time we had heavy rain, the septic overflowed. Now, I must have missed the "How to manage an overflowing septic system on a school site 101" at principal school; I had never dealt with a septic before, though I soon learnt. If you had a recording of my first phone call with the plumber, it would have sounded something like: "So the toilet pit seems to have bubbles coming out of one of the lids and there is a pipe with a few bends that also seems to be making some noises". The plumber arrived with little idea of the issue. In a very short time, and after a few floods, my language adapted to support my communication with the experts on the issue: "The septic is overflowing again due to the stormwater runoff. The third and fourth chambers seem to have been affected, with the overflow pipe clogging on the first elbow". I felt very "tradey", though I am sure I still have a lot of work to do on my septic talk. However, the language was more specific and the plumber was able to gain some understanding of the problem before arriving and therefore be prepared for the task.

What is essential is that in every organisation there is a language of learning. When we are leading improvement, it is crucial that every member of our team is included in that specific narrative. It is even more crucial that the story is not completed by leadership; they may have the draft beginning and a predicted end, but there should be an opportunity for all staff to be involved in the development and completion of the story. Just as important is that we agree on the language of improvement. So, if by chance during our improvement process the septic starts to overflow, we will all have a common language to explicitly explain the issue so that leaders and other team members can step in to help to resolve the problem before it becomes too big.

There will still be occasions – like when I called the plumbers – when we will need further investigation, and possibly we will have to pivot and introduce some additional language or conversation to support a deviation in the improvement process. We cannot be static with our direction and lose the opportunity to add value to the narrative. As Covey (1989) argues, "seek first to understand, then be understood". Potentially the diversion of common language in the improvement story may simply be a misinterpretation of the existing narrative. Possibly, this may be an opportunity for further adult learning if a misconception has been made evident, one that may be isolated to an individual or a team or may be something that needs to be addressed as an organisation. Or this may be an opportunity for organisational learning and improvement – an opportunity to add value to the improvement strategy.

Defour and Fullan suggest that systems will have greater consistency, sustained improvement, and better responsiveness to improvement processes, while building the capacity and ability of more individuals and teams to become improvement leaders, when we ensure we have more staff who can "talk the walk" while also being able to "walk the talk" (2013, p. 31). Proposing this means that you have a common vocabulary or language that your teams can articulate while believing in the purpose and rationale, goals, targets and strategy. Most importantly, they need to be able do this with a consistent voice.

Leadership reflection task

- ☐ Can you think of a time when language has been used (intentionally or unintentionally) that left you feeling excluded?
- ☐ What intentional language do you use in your organisation to ensure all members of your community feel included?
- ☐ When leading improvement, do you consider the specific intentional language you want to use and want to avoid?

CHAPTER 12
What if it doesn't work?

The big question, which can often take up a lot of a leader's energy and brain space, is what do I do if I have implemented the SKIM Model – or any improvement model, framework or process for that matter – and I still have a staff member who will not budge? They have continued to disregard the opportunities and exposure to the improvement strategy. Throughout your implementation of the SKIM Model, this staff member – let's call him Steve – has had the opportunity to be actively involved in the Meerkat Effect, which has supported the development of the improvement vision, goals, and targets. He has seen the Success Team build momentum through the initial execution of the improvement process. He has completed numerous adult learning sessions where his colleagues have celebrated and presented their individual and team successes and barriers. Steve has observed the Knowledge and Inquisitive Teams demonstrating their progress and he has had opportunities to be directly involved in robust discussion and feedback. Running parallel have been high-impact improvement strategies, such as instructional coaching, peer observations and individual and team support with resources or further adult learning access. However, Steve is still not engaging in the improvement process.

The difficulty we are always confronted with is that we have a range of people with a range of responses based on many varying factors, some of which are extremely entrenched in their history. As Defour and Fullan (2013) argue, there are two undeniable facts with change: it is achievable; however, it is unquestionably difficult. We know we cannot force people to accept change or a new improvement direction. Moreover, we will get limited traction by attempting to persuade or manipulate the situation and convince people like Steve to get on board. There is a common leadership by-product that may present itself as we start to consider how we approach this resistant staff member. I must reiterate that in any change or improvement strategy, conflict or perceived conflict is part of the improvement puzzle. Nevertheless, as we get to the minority of staff, and if one or a few are presenting with further challenge or resistance, we can start to default to an emotive response: this staff member is simply "trying to be difficult"; they are purposely "trying to make my job harder".

It is at this point that we can lose empathy and balance, which in turn can fracture relationships, making progress even harder. As Fullan (2010) writes in his book *Motion Leadership: The Skinny on Becoming Change Savvy*, "handling resistance and building relationships are part and parcel of the same strategy" (2010, p. 73). Fullan (2010) also proposes that if you are "savvy" in leading improvement, more importantly, in building relationships and understanding the people you lead, then a framework such as the SKIM Model can reduce or even eliminate opposition. Successful execution of the Meerkat Effect will expose the early potential of opposition before you have completed your implementation of the SKIM Model. We also must acknowledge that the "Steves" of our workplace have a genuine reason for why they are behaving the way they are. There is always a chance that there is a level of truth to their narrative if we take the time to listen and understand. Macklin and Zbar (2020) reference a significant analysis of staff development and change published by Guskey, where it was found that "we change behaviour if we want to change beliefs" (1983, p. 5). Therefore, if we want to have any degree of change with our resistant staff members, we must understand what the source of their behaviour is.

It is not personal

The SKIM Model is one that is based on the best intentions for every member of our team, every person we are leading, big (staff or community) or small (students). They must all have their leader's optimistic attention.

Optimism is a leadership superpower and one that is contagious in our organisations. Like our body language or dispositions, when we are engaging with our teams, optimism is one of our loudest voices. Staff can feel your enthusiasm; they will mirror your passionate approach, and the members of staff who are showing any level of resistance will be watching and awaiting your response to decide if you are going to enter a battle or if you will raise the white flag in surrender. My challenge to you is not to do either. Instead of standing on the battlefield facing off, or throwing in the towel where neither the leader, the resistant staff member, nor the students will come out victorious, why not stand on their side of the field? Stand next to them and take in their view, from their perspective, getting an understanding of why it is that they are in this position. It may not fully resolve the resistance, but it will strengthen the trust and relationship to move forward.

My belief is that when we are leading improvement, we sometimes can unnecessarily take on the improvement process as a personal reflection of our leadership success. I would argue that in the case of leading improvement through the SKIM Model, a leader's error in this situation is to have created conflict based on their own beliefs around the improvement agenda. We should be leading with the beliefs of our organisation, in which our beliefs along with those of our staff are embedded. If there is conflict or resistance, this should not be because of our beliefs but based on those of the organisation and those of the people that we are leading.

The SKIM Model reflects our context and the people we are leading. If there is resistance to the improvement process, it is highly likely that the focus of the dispute is the bigger improvement focus, rather than a reflection of any individual. The alternative is that there is a fractured relationship between the leader and the member being led, in which case that relationship must be the priority of the improvement effort before all else. Munby suggests that when you feel under fire or hesitant in leadership, focus on three key ideas: "hold your core values, go back to the people management approaches that have worked well for you in the past, be an enthusiastic but focused learner" (2019, p. 179). This is also supported by Heifetz and Linsky (2002), who propose that effective leadership is being on the dance floor, being an active learner and an engaged member of the team, while also being on the balcony, getting the big picture view to support the management and leadership decisions holistically. Traditional styles of leadership may have involved spending the majority of time on the balcony, managing and leading from a hierarchical viewpoint. However, it is well documented, and supported by research, that the best and most effective leaders lead alongside their staff.

Unintentional avoidance

A natural response to perceived conflict is avoidance, and this can occur in many ways, some of which are unintentional. When we feel there is the potential for conflict, we can subconsciously retreat, finding a bookshelf in a hidden corner to rearrange as the person enters our environment. If we are in a position of cognitive overload, or our emotional state is feeling battered, human nature is to go into protective made. There is a perceived danger approaching; we will either flee, fight or freeze. If we know or become aware of a challenge, it is important to reflect on our response as leaders. Are we avoiding the space? In reality, if we want it to improve, we need to spend time in the spaces that we find the most challenging. We will learn more and mend more.

I recall a period of time when I was leading a school and I was getting daily phone calls concerning complaints, unresolved issues, and perceptions about the level of communication. These calls were from a consistent group of parents. I was a little confused, because we had, I believed, a good process in place for following up any issues or incidents. However, there must have been a gap in the process, because seemingly these families did not feel like they were getting sufficient communication. The other interesting factor was that the families' children were all in different grades; there seemed to be a consistent disconnection between school and home.

I met with my team with curiosity to discuss the process and find where we were going wrong. I soon noticed, after my individual conversations with the staff involved and a collective discussion about our communication process, that some of the follow-up was being avoided, since the perception was that every phone call or conversation with these particular families turned into a conflict. In fact, this had a level of truth, due to the relationships being damaged and getting further harmed with every missed opportunity to connect with the family. Following this discovery, I designed a learning and reflection session with our staff. I asked each staff member to think of one family or person that they were considerably challenged by. I got each of the team to write down the last three to five conversations they had had with this person, including the topic of the conversation and any brief details they could recall. We then all had to look at the list and reflect on the overall themes that had been identified. What did we notice?

In almost all cases, the last three to five conversations, if not all, had a negative theme – a behavioural issue, an injury, being late back to class, not following reasonable instructions. It was clear why the relationship was fractured. Because we perceived every conversation as a challenge or conflict, we were avoiding communication unless it was absolutely necessary, which in most cases was because there was an issue or incident that we had no choice but to communicate. The only time the family was hearing from the teacher was for a negative reason. Therefore, the parent was getting on the front foot to get in first, and calling to complain about any incident, true or embellished, that the child was bringing home.

It was one of those "aha" moment for my team. We set some goals around identifying students, not just the ones above, whose families we had not communicated with for a period of time. Then we simply called them to have a chat about something positive that had occurred in their child's learning, in their social connections, or just because they were being a positive member of our community – to catch them being good and celebrate it. The result was immediate, with one parent crying on the phone because it was the first positive thing they had heard from the school that year – a sad but accurate reality. The relationship was not mended, but we had put a little bit of silicon in the gap to stop the leaking. It is important to consistently ensure we are building good relationships through positive communication and connections. As with leading teams and individuals, we cannot expect each to respond positively if they are not feeling as though they are treated positively. It is our responsibility as leaders to connect with our staff, not theirs as those being led.

Adult learning theories agree that we learn most from being faced with problems and challenges to overcome. This is no different from learning to be a more effective leader. Throughout the examples and stories in this book that I have used to demonstrate the SKIM Model's effectiveness, I have continued to highlight my mistakes, or the challenges I have confronted. These are what have supported the adaption and refinement of the SKIM Model over my leadership journey. Tim Bighthouse (National College for Teaching and Leadership, 2015) suggests there are four attributes a leader requires to lead change effectively:

1. Regard crisis as the norm and complexity as the fun – learn how to feel good in stressful situations.
2. A bottomless well of intellectual curiosity.
3. A complete absence of paranoia and self-pity – be vulnerable.
4. Unwarranted optimism.

Only you have the power to determine how you will feel about and approach any situation. This power, when flexed for unwavering positive regard towards the people you are leading, will have the most remarkable and significant impact on those people. You can choose to see complexity as a problem. However, as we have discussed, we learn best when faced with a problem. Lean into the problem with curiosity and optimism. Model as a leader how you confront difficulties with vulnerability, enjoyment, and confidence, because that is the space where we will do the most learning and come out the other side a fuller leader.

Maslow's hierarchy of needs theory (1966) highlights the complexities of humans, and particularly that we are not one-dimensional. Maslow identifies that prior to "self-actualisation" which is the achievement of an individual's potential, there are four other needs that must be met:

1. Psychological needs – food, water, rest
2. Safety needs – shelter, security, safety
3. Social needs – friends, relationships
4. Esteem needs – prestige and accomplishment.

All of these needs must be met prior to achieving our potential. As a leader, there are some of these that we will struggle to have a direct influence on and others that we may be able to influence, depending on our organisation's context.

However, understanding your staff members' circumstances will support the decisions and empathy you can lead with. I can think of one staff member many years ago who started to present differently at work. A colleague had noticed this and dropped into my office to raise some concern. After touching base with the staff member, I found that they were working through some personal relationship challenges and a lot of uncertainty when they got home after work. This simple understanding changed how I responded and led this staff member. They still had to meet professional and context expectation within their role and team; however, I could adapt my approach so that I was not adding to their already uncertain and challenging world.

Where is the line?

I must be clear, the SKIM Model is an improvement framework; it is not a performance management process. In leadership, the water can become murky when we are into the latter stages of an improvement cycle, when we have engaged the Measured Team and are now focusing on the final, small percentage of staff who have yet to commit or even comply with the improvement strategy. The murkiness comes from, as discussed earlier in this chapter, situations where we take the improvement challenge personally or at least as a reflection of our process and leadership. In *Open-to-Learning Leadership: How to Build Trust While Tackling Tough Issues*, Robinson et al. suggest that "principals commonly struggle to have effective conversations about staff performance issues, tending to tolerate, protect, and work around such issues rather than effectively addressing them" (2016, p. 131). Robinson (2016) comments further that leadership has the challenge of maintaining a balance between exercising influence and leading ongoing improvement, while establishing and maintaining effective relationships. This balance can complicate performance management follow-up because there is the potential to damage or fracture these relationships by causing worry or defensiveness in your staff and potentially in yourself.

Before you consider performance management, you should ensure that:

- You have considered all other factors and removed all obstacles that may have become present.
- You have sought advice and had discussions, both informal and formal, with the staff member and addressed any potential supports and resource issues that may have arisen.

- You are clear that you, as the leader, are not the barrier and that you have solicited non-biased advice from a trusted colleague.
- You have, as Robinson et al. (2016) have described, considered and approached any performance issue or any discussion that has the potential to damage a relationship with open-mindedness and respect that is genuine, thus increasing the potential for a quick, collaborative and sustained resolution to the concerns.

If all these things have been considered and reasonably enacted with a minimal result or an improvement that still is not meeting expectations, the next potential option to consider is undeniably difficult. It will take a significant amount of courage, planning and evidence. It is a role every leader must take extremely seriously and with a high level of vigilance and transparency. It is at this point that you may need to consider performance management. There would be very few organisations that do not have a formal performance management process and policy to support the direction and decisions that need to be made. It is essential that however the process is formed, it is followed with precision.

The consequences of getting this wrong can be damaging for the staff member, the culture of the organisation and the credibility of the leader. As Kouzes and Posner (2012) put it, strong leaders show consistency between their words and actions. They don't only stand up for what they believe in; they model and practise what they preach. They demonstrate expectation not by words but by actions and commitment to the values that have been agreed upon. Credibility comes from visible actions, not from words. The other staff are most likely aware of their colleague's resistance and have seen the challenges, be they appropriate questioning or inappropriate undermining. Everyone would have heard the saying "The problem you walk past is the problem you accept" or something similar. The decisions you make when faced with underperformance, or staff who are not meeting the minimum standards, will be viewed and, in many ways, judged by your other staff to determine what is an acceptable level of professionalism and what is not. A leader's credibility, based on accepting or challenging unprofessional or underperforming staff, can be strengthened or damaged.

A great starting point in Australia is the Australian Institute for Teaching and School Leadership (AITSL) Standards. These are considered the minimum professional standards for teachers and leaders in the Australian system. It is here that I can identify the areas that are in deficit and begin to formalise a process based on supporting evidence and the policy outlined by the organisation's administrators. In the education system in every state, there would also be a code of conduct or code of ethics. This is established through the organisation's governance and generally focused on a set of values and expectations that all staff must adhere to. The support documents, along with the relevant policy, will provide the foundation for how, when, and if you will need to follow a performance management process, or if there is another option to consider. At the end of the day, I want the best people standing in front of the students in my community. If any member of the team is not meeting the expectations of our culture or organisation, it is my responsibility as the leader to address this, in the interests of everyone but ultimately of the young minds they stand in front of and influence each day.

Leadership reflection task

Unintentional avoidance:

- ☐ Consider a person within your community that you are challenged by.
- ☐ What have been the last three conversations or interactions you have had with them?
- ☐ How would you represent the interactions (positive/negative/neutral)?
- ☐ How might you mend or minimise the challenge through engaging in a different way or through deliberate interactions?

CHAPTER 13

Research of influence

The empirical research around leadership is significant and is not showing any signs of slowing down. Leadership impacts almost every organisation, therefore mastery of leadership is the source of superior accomplishment and outcomes in personal and professional pursuits of excellence. I am not going to attempt to do a meta-analysis of leadership investigations and studies over the decades here. Instead, I will address a few key pieces that supported the development of the SKIM Model, some of which challenged my initial thinking, and some of which are questioned by the SKIM Model.

If you look at the abundance of leadership research, there is still a noticeable gap between the capabilities that a good leader needs to develop to become a great leader, and how to implement these capabilities in order to have the greatest positive impact on your organisation. The SKIM Model is one of the frameworks that aims to fill this gap. It doesn't need a particular person at the helm, it doesn't require advanced skills, and it is not determined by the context in which you are leading. It is a framework where leaders can lean into their strengths and model vulnerability about their areas for improvement. A well-rounded leader is not one who has all the necessary skills and capabilities and can implement these effectively and at the right time. Instead, I believe that a well-rounded leader is one who is self-aware and can acknowledge that they do not always have the expertise or evidence.

They are also aware of others' strengths and their environment and lean on the people in the best position to ensure a great outcome for all.

The first skim

Coming out of the peak of the Covid-19 pandemic, I had taken on a system leader role. An opportunity to review and revise our adult learning architecture presented itself to our network executive team, and we collectively decided it was time for an evaluation of how and why we work together as a network of principals. The improvement was built around a simple phrase: "Every principal should leave a network meeting feeling like it was a valuable use of their time". None of us have enough time to waste, so a meeting cannot be wasted time. This phrase challenged the agenda, the presentations, the purpose, and the planning.

As Priya Parker, author of *The Art of Gathering: How We Meet and Why It Matters* (2018) argues, people connect through meaningful discussions; any time a leader brings a group of people together, the purpose must be transparent. The meeting must establish meaningful opportunities for people to connect to why they are there and more importantly a common purpose that encourages dialogue with each other. Collectively, we redesigned a learning structure that not only got traction locally, but also received attention at a state level, with several other principal networks seeking direction and support to have a similar influence on their local networks and systems' learning architecture. Although I hold a lot of pride in this system level opportunity to lead improvement, with an outstanding team that led this work alongside me, it started me pondering, "What does my personal leadership architecture look like?" I could explain the process I use, I could provide several examples of how it has worked or how I "got it wrong", learnt from my errors, and built my own leadership capacity as a result. But I could not easily show anyone, and for me that is important in learning and understanding any new concept. If a colleague was to share with me their leadership model, I would need to see it, draw it, visualise it, trial it before I could confidently say, "I get it". It's a little like Benjamin Franklin's famous quote, "Tell me and I forget, teach me and I may remember, involve me and I learn".

Consequently I went on a search for a model that represented how I lead, how I involve my staff, and how I have a relentless positive regard for my people. In my search, I was seeking a model that was inclusive and involved everyone yet communicated a degree of "permission" to invest energy in places where I would get maximum output or traction. Many of the models I found were a series of dot points, very complex visuals, or a framework that I personally just could not connect with. Thus, I developed the SKIM Model.

Where does the SKIM Model fit?

One of the initial and most renowned leading change models I examined was Dr John Kotter's "8 Steps for Leading Change". Kotter has spent years researching different organisations to discover why some of these organisations outperform others. What are the leaders of change doing differently or consistently to ensure they are strong agents of leading change? From this extensive research, Kotter published the book *Leading Change* (1996) and identified eight key steps that were common across the successful organisations that were effective in positively leading change.

Figure 11: Kotter's 8-step Change Model

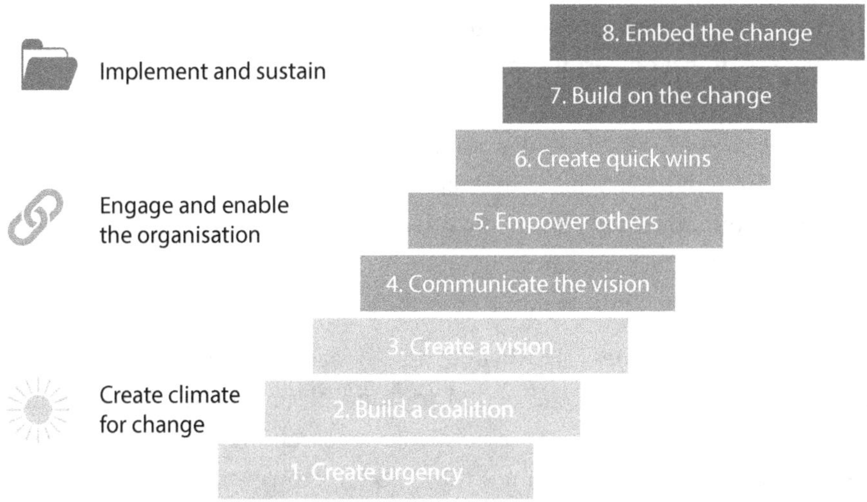

Implement and sustain
- 8. Embed the change
- 7. Build on the change

Engage and enable the organisation
- 6. Create quick wins
- 5. Empower others
- 4. Communicate the vision

Create climate for change
- 3. Create a vision
- 2. Build a coalition
- 1. Create urgency

The model version in Figure 11 shows the process as a step-by-step plan. The Kotter International Inc. website (2024) explains the 8-Step Change Model as follows:

1. **Create a sense of urgency** – inspire people to act.
2. **Build a guiding coalition** – a volunteer network of committed people to guide it, coordinate it, and communicate its activities.
3. **Form a strategic vision** – clarify how the future will be different from the past.
4. **Enlist a volunteer army** – large-scale change can only occur when massive numbers of people rally around a common purpose.
5. **Enable action by removing barriers** – remove obstacles that slow things down or create roadblocks to progress.
6. **Generate short-term wins** – wins are the molecules of results. They must be recognised, collected, and communicated.
7. **Sustain acceleration** – be relentless with initiating change after change until the vision is a reality.
8. **Institute change** – articulate the connection between new behaviours and organisational success, making sure they continue until they become strong enough to replace old habits.

Kotter's 8 steps are supported by common errors displayed by organisations that are not as effective (as cited in Dinham, 2008, p. 128):

1. Not establishing a great enough sense of urgency.
2. Not creating a powerful enough guiding coalition.
3. Lacking vision.
4. Under-communicating the vision.
5. Not removing obstacles to the new vision.
6. Not systematically planning for and creating short-term wins.
7. Declaring victory too soon.
8. Not anchoring changes in the corporation's culture.

The SKIM Model does not dispute the decades of trials, reviews and research that Kotter has completed in building and refining this model. If fact, the SKIM Model complements the research, most of which can be found scattered throughout the SKIM Model. However, I would question the implication that the 8 steps must be taken in the specified order. From my experience in leading people (who, as we have established, are complex beings), I would argue that there may be movement up or down the 8 steps depending on where your staff needs lie. For example, "Communicate the Vision" (step 4) cannot be a one-off; it needs to be repeated and refined in an ongoing manner. Through deconstructing Kotter's model, and aligning it with the SKIM Model, I was able to reflect the significant amount of research through a more simple and malleable framework, the SKIM Model.

Figure 12: The SKIM Model reflecting Kotter's 8-Step Change Model

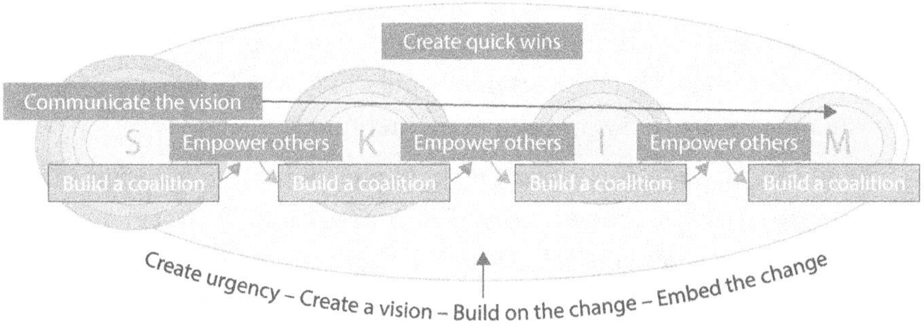

Figure 12 reflects Kotter's 8-Step Change Model, deconstructed to demonstrate the links to the SKIM Model. It does not challenge the research behind Kotter's model; instead, it has adapted the research to show a different way to implement, lead change, and more to the point, lead improvement. The reconstruction is explained using the language from Figure 11.

- **Create quick wins** – This sits nicely within the Meerkat Effect – a space of celebration and communication of the success of each of the teams. But also there are a series of other important roles the Meerkat Effect reveals.
- **Create urgency, create a vision, build on the change, embed the change** – These are also embedded in the Meerkat Effect process. It is important that all staff are constantly exposed to the improvement evolution. We are not working in the background with doors closed while the rest of the team wait for their opportunity to get exposure to what is happening. By the time we engage each individual member of the team with their opportunity to join a SKIM team, they have already had the reason for the urgency or need communicated, they have had

genuine input and feedback into the improvement vision, they have clearly seen the incremental steps building on the improvements and change strategy, they have seen the evidence and how this has improved the desired outcome, and commitment follows.

- **Communicate the vision** – All staff need to be a part of the vision creation; however, the Success Team will be the team initially responsible for demonstrating the vision in action. The momentum will build from their success and the following teams will have their opportunity to showcase their impact on the vision's success.

- **Build a coalition** – The SKIM teams are your coalition, starting with the Success Team and then intentionally building the subsequent teams with the increase in improvement momentum.

- **Empower others** – This is on repeat; we are continuously leading our teams to empower the next team. This process doesn't stop in the SKIM Model; it starts from the selection of the Success Team, empowering them with the responsibility, resources, support and skills to empower others – leadership that leads leaders to lead.

The deconstruction of Kotter's 8-Step Change Model provides a different level of flexibility and roundness in your process. Everyone is involved from the very beginning and continues to be involved until you are happy with the desired outcome. There are no surprises or "gotcha" moments hidden around the corner. Ultimately, this will build a level of trust and a collaborative culture in improvement opportunities.

Innovation

Everett Rogers' "Diffusion of Innovation" theory (1962) is a sociological theory based on research that explains how a product, idea or technology gains momentum over time and then spreads through a population or social system (diffusion). Rogers found that the diffusion process does not happen simultaneously over a population, but is activated within one group at a time. Rogers separated the people impacted by an innovation into five groups (see Figure 13).

Figure 13: Everett Rogers' Diffusion of Innovation curve

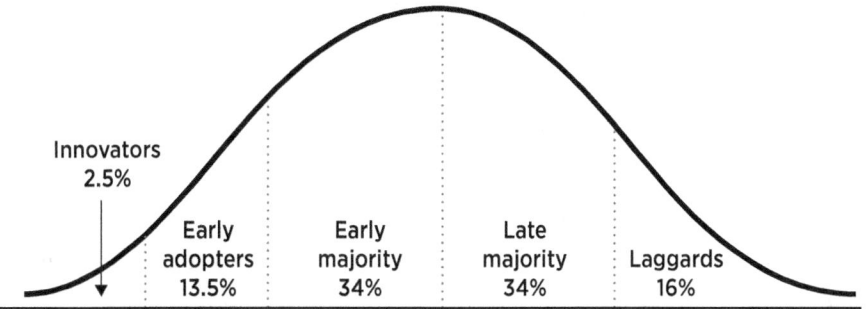

- **Innovators** – These are often the first to engage with a new idea or innovation. They are happy to take risks and will often place a lot of trust in their leaders. Very little needs to be done to attract the innovators to adopt and trial change or improvement.
- **Early adopters** – These people are often aware of the need for change and can often take on leadership roles. They need a little more information than the innovators. They do not need a lot of convincing to embrace change and improvement. They often love an information sheet showing the highlights of the direction, evidence and proposed outcomes.
- **Early majority** – Often this category needs to see evidence that the change or improvement strategy works before accepting the challenge. They rarely would put their hand up to lead but are happy to pursue improvement once they have sufficient details.
- **Late majority** – These are often your sceptics. They need a strong case to adopt change and improvement. They will often need to see a lot of evidence and modelling of the strategy or expectations before considering engaging. They require additional support, resources and reassurance.
- **Laggards** – This group is seen as the hardest people to get on board to any change or improvement. They are often caught in historical trials. They may begin by being compliant and limited to surface level implementation before committing. These people may only engage once there is no other option.

Rogers' theory is a great way to understand the rough percentages of staff that may fit into any of the above categories. However, like any bell curve that has been based on a significant portion of a population, these numbers are reflective of averages rather than being an exact science. The other limitation with this theory is that it doesn't link strategy with category. It identifies the groupings based on behavioural types, but how do I implement strategies to best influence each group?

Although Rogers' model suggests that a new innovation spreads through a population by "diffusion", the spreading of momentum doesn't happen naturally by osmosis, as we have demonstrated throughout this book. Diffusion occurs through strategic planning and implementation by leadership with intentional direction, vision and a clear destination. If we consider one of the most influential brands in technology over the last few decades, Apple, the use of the product, along with its diffusion throughout populations across the globe, did not just happen. It was intentional advertising and brand marketing that built the momentum and uptake of the technology. Simon Sinek's book *Start with Why* (2009) and his corresponding TED Talk explain in very simple terms the effective marketing strategy that created the momentum or diffusion across an international population. Early on, Apple did not offer a lot of difference or have more of a qualification than other brands to build phones or computers. Their clever, strategic marketing and planning built the momentum and the diffusion through a worldwide population.

Diffusion of the SKIM Model

Figure 14 overlays the SKIM Model on top of the Diffusion of Innovation curve. The themes from Rogers' model are not in dispute; the significant difference is that there are no clear lines to identify percentages of staff within each SKIM team – and that is on purpose. The SKIM Model is adaptable and flexible based on any context in which it is implemented.

We must remember that in leading improvement we want to build teams with the right people, not the easy people. In Rogers' theory, the innovators arguably need little or no encouragement to support and lead the change or improvement. If you have any staff on your team who fall into that category, you will see that they are often the first to put their hands up for almost any improvement or directional change. This also implies that they are risk-takers; it is important to have some of these staff in your staff room, but they may need to have their enthusiasm harnessed to ensure that the risks they take are not in opposition to the vision and direction – that they are measured risks that leadership is happy to support. We know we learn through making errors, and risk-taking is where we can often make some of the best innovative decisions, but it is also where we can make many mistakes. This is not a negative; it is just something we need to understand and respond appropriately to. I will reiterate: are these innovative staff always the right people? We don't need to push back on the innovator's enthusiasm; however, reflecting on "Context, Capacity, Culture" (see Figure 6, page 60), it is highly likely, due to their eagerness, that they will have other improvement opportunities they are supporting or involved in or may be better suited to – but if not, and they are the right person, then get their energy on board.

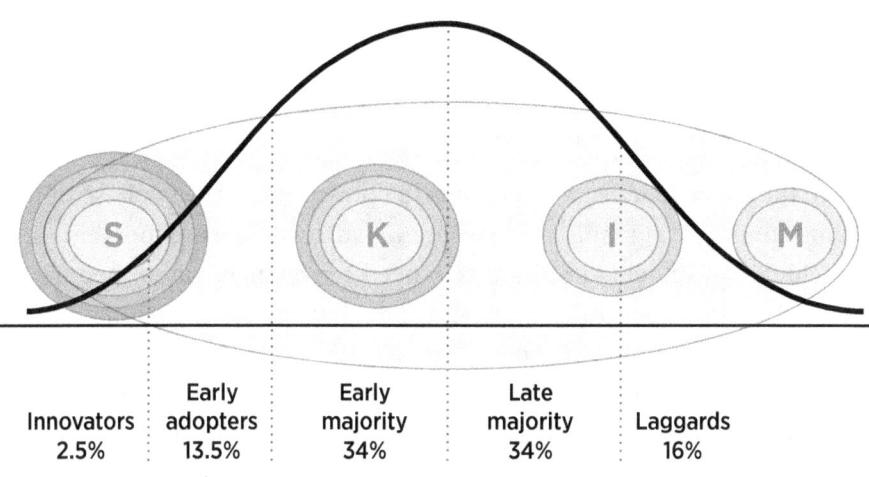

Figure 14: Diffusion of the SKIM Model

I would challenge some of Rogers' language. The word "laggard" conflicts with the positive intent of the SKIM Model. "Laggard" is defined as someone or something that is very slow to adopt. I personally perceive that language as a negative label, and much prefer "measured". However, whether laggard or measured, we have established that we have to change behaviours before we can change beliefs, and although the Diffusion of Innovation curve doesn't provide a model to support any of Rogers' categories, I would argue that I am a better leader with these "very slow to adopt" staff in my staff room, asking questions, challenging thinking, and ensuring I am well prepared when I walk into the adult learning session.

What else?

James Prochaska and his colleagues at the University of Rhode Island (Prochaska et al., 1994; cited in Knight, 2011) conducted more than 55 clinical studies of more than 1000 people attempting to make major changes in their lives. The result greatly helped understand how people experience and manage significant change in their lives. They argue that change involves six stages:

1. Pre-contemplation, when we are unaware of our need for change.
2. Contemplation, when we weigh the advantages and disadvantages of changing to a new way of doing something.
3. Preparation, when we prepare to implement change.
4. Action, when we implement change.
5. Maintenance, when we sustain our implementation plan.
6. Termination, when we are no longer changing because we have completed the change process.

Often the space of most contention is the pre-contemplation phase of this change theory. It is in this space where we are leading team members and individuals to understand there is a need for change. Often, people do not realise they need to change, and that is where a leader's intentional strategy can build momentum and be taken on as a positive opportunity – or can have an adverse effect if the need for change is not appropriately communicated. Those who are not aware of their need for change have time and space in the SKIM Model to build their understanding and acceptance of the inevitability and necessity of the looming change or improvement. Effective activation of the Meerkat Effect will support the development of a collective staff understanding of improvement. It also takes the focus away from "I need to improve", which can seem personal and be interpreted as a negative improvement strategy by the staff member, to "We need to improve" as a collective, which acknowledges that every individual has a significant part to play in that improvement process.

Smith (2005, pp. 408-9) identifies three key steps to support a readiness for change, which have similar language to Kotter's 8-Step Change Model:

1. Creating a sense of need and urgency.
2. Communicating the change message and ensuring participation and involvement in the change process.
3. Providing anchoring points and a base for the achievement of change.

Smith argues that if there is going to be any form of organisational change, the leaders need to ensure that the people who ultimately have the greatest impact on the success of the change or improvement process are prepared for the change. The SKIM Model effectively saves time in ensuring that staff are ready. We have acknowledged that "readiness" comes at different times and with different criteria for each individual staff member or team. Through the Meerkat Effect, readiness is built through collective capacity building. The staff are not pushed to be ready before their awaited entrance into their appropriate SKIM Team. Readiness must be respected and developed; more importantly, readiness must be effectively led. Supporting Smith's approach to readiness for change, McLagen (2002) argues that if there is a lack of readiness, some fundamental organisational change literature will support readiness, emphasising that participation, information, education, communication, involvement, support and agreement are all necessary. McLagen offers five strategies that support successful readiness (2002, pp. 44-45):

1. Be sure the change adds value.
2. Match the change process with the change.
3. Provide management support.
4. Prepare the system for change.
5. Help people align to the change agenda.

Smith (2005), McLagen (2002) and Prochaska et al. (1994) all provide a language of change that may be different in words but has similar meaning in process – the key principles that are necessary or that we need to avoid to ensure successful improvement or change or prevent a failed attempt. The notable gap is that implementation of the key theories is open to interpretation. No leader enters an improvement process hoping to fail or come across significant roadblocks. I will argue that we can plan for improvement; the research is supportive across many theories of action – what works and what doesn't in leading improvement.

The Queensland Education Leadership Institute (QELI, 2017) developed a leadership framework that Macklin and Zbar reviewed, contending that this framework comprises knowledge, understanding, attitudes, skills and personal qualities. Macklin and Zbar suggest that the five leadership elements in this framework enable the leader to perform at a high level in their role, while identifying key actions that need to be taken to ensure ongoing improvement in their schools. The five identified elements are (2020, p. 23):

1. Diagnosing performance and prescribing for improvement.
2. Developing leadership to drive improvement.
3. Ensuring effective implementation of what matters most.
4. Leveraging the greatest source of improvement in schools.
5. Ensuring progress and keeping on track.

The five identified elements are perfect examples of strategic processing from leadership. Each of the five elements has a detailed description of the possible considerations for each of the individual elements. This example of an improvement framework, which every state education system would have a version of, can run consecutively with the SKIM Model. The SKIM Model sets the structure for the leader to implement strong leadership in improvement. The improvement framework can be used as a tool or resource for each of the SKIM teams to investigate the improvement strategy at a team level, and to then use this as the tool to celebrate and discuss challenges with the rest of the staff within the Meerkat Effect.

Whichever model you choose to implement to support leading improvement, you must consider how the people you lead fit into the chosen model and how the model supports the people you lead. Improvement cannot occur without the support and engagement of your staff – they are the vehicle for any form of improvement. How are you going to engage them? How are you going to bring them along for an enjoyable journey of improvement? These are questions that no amount of data or leadership studies will answer. We know that improvement and change are crucial for every organisation, particularly schools – and the leader is the conductor of the orchestra. It is the leader's responsibility to make sure that all musicians are reading the same music, are on the same page at the same time, and know exactly when it is their turn to play to create a beautiful piece of music that every single person in the community is proud of.

Leadership reflection task

- [ ] What research has had the greatest impact on your leadership?
- [ ] How has it shaped or challenged the way you lead?
- [ ] What model/process do you use when leading improvement?

CHAPTER 14
Conclusion

Is it broken?

This is a question that helps when my leadership team or staff and I are talking about a perceived urgency. I intentionally use the language "perceived urgency" because I have found over my leadership career that there are very few situations where there is a genuine urgency to take action immediately. To be honest, urgency can often fall within a safety realm; something has presented as unsafe, therefore we need to make a decision quickly to minimise the risk. Often the urgency in improvement is a combination of top-down pressure to get the results and internal organisational pressure to have the evidence of improvement, while also juggling a lot of balls in the area of targets or improvement goals. The purpose of the question "Is it broken?" is to allow a level of reflection before making quick, hasty and possibly damaging decisions around the improvement process. If you did absolutely nothing today, left everything as status quo, would the teaching and learning continue as it is tomorrow? Would anyone be at risk in terms of their psychological or physical safety? If they are, it is not the SKIM Model process that is required, but if they are not, and everyone will be OK, why rush? You have the privilege and difficult responsibility to set the tone, direction and pace. As Hattie states, "so often, we spend too much time on saying what leaders ought to be, ought to do, and ought to value; instead, we need to spend more time considering how to effectively create schools in which leaders are responsible for, allow, and encourage all to know about and have positive impacts on student learning" (2012, p. 178).

Sustained improvement cannot be achieved with speedy short-term planning and thinking. As I discussed above, it is better to slow the process and pace, and lead improvement the right way, not the easy way. If improvement was easy, there would not be so much research about how to do it effectively – our jobs as leaders would be a breeze. Acknowledge the required slow pace of implementation, and if what is currently in place is not broken, we don't have to take immediate action. This is easy to say; however, it takes ongoing practice, a level of resilience, self-awareness, activation of your rational brain, and a substantial amount of training of your emotional brain, before you can confidently and consistently look at a situation and pending improvement process and say, "It is OK. We do not need to rush this".

The power lies with the leaders, and as the French author Voltaire once said, "With great power comes great responsibility". The responsibility you have with any sustained improvement process is to get results without overloading your staff. The first and most important step, as we highlighted earlier in the book, is to say yes to only the right initiatives or strategies and say no to everything else. Be fussy and demand only the best opportunities for your organisation.

You set the pace

When I hung up my umpiring whistle, I had left a semi-professional environment. We had a structured six-days-a-week program, skin-fold assessments, and fitness time trials, both pre-season and mid-season. We had access to a team of physiotherapists, osteopaths, dietitians and trainers for rubdowns and strapping. It was an intense, semi-professional athletic environment with high standards of performance on the track and field. A few years after retiring, although I had continued running, I was not enjoying my regular runs. I was feeling worse after the run and my motivation to stay active was depleting. My once highly enjoyable and physically rewarding running capability was having the opposite effect mentally. I was also noticing an unusual flatness in my daily behaviours and routines. Energy levels were low, enthusiasm was fluctuating, and I started to feel a level of concern about my mental health. I wasn't feeling like me, or more accurately, I wasn't feeling like the old version of me.

I made an appointment to see a psychologist to try and figure out a pathway back to some balance in my physical, psychological and emotional world. After a few sessions, we started to investigate my intrinsically competitive nature. I was in a high-performing role as a school leader, I had been in a high-performing athletic space, I was a dad and husband and attempting to execute my home life at the same high standards. I set myself high targets and aspirations and always tried to be the best at whatever I set out to do. However, I was attempting to be the best in every facet of my world, so I was spreading myself too thin and was paying the price emotionally.

One of our initial discussions revolved around my loss of love of going for what I considered a leisurely jog. We investigated what this jog looked like. In short, I would set out on my run, setting myself a reasonable pace. As I was running, I would continuously look at my watch, notice that I was running 5 or 10 seconds faster than my intended pace, then adjust my goal to the faster pace and keep running. Soon I would look again and notice I was running 5 or 10 seconds faster than my adjusted pace, so again I would reset my goal pace and step it up again. By the end of the run, I was spent. I did not enjoy the run and felt like every run was a time trial. What we concluded was I had physically retired from my six-days-a-week training schedule, but mentally I was still pursuing that level of fitness. My mind was overpowering my body as I ran. Looking at my watch, I would be mentally saying, "Steve, what is this you are dishing up? This is not quick enough; you can run quicker than this" and so I did. I felt like I was competing in a race every run, but the reality was I was only racing myself – there was no one else, there was no competition.

In order to crack this mindset, I started to take control of the pace, simply by not wearing my GPS watch when I ran. I knew the distance of the track, but without my watch I had no idea of the pace; instead I had to listen to my body, run at a pace that was comfortable. And I did not know how long it took until I got home. Now I cannot just switch off the competitive nature within me, but what taking my GPS watch off did was completely change my mindset and retrain my brain to control my pace based on a consideration of multiple factors, like listening to my body, not just time and pace. The results were substantial and I felt more present and calm during my runs, apart from when I had to zigzag past an owner walking their dog on the right-hand side, resulting in the dog taking over the path (still an ongoing issue I have to work through). In fact, any time I felt a little stuck writing this book, a quick run cleared any fogginess.

This example demonstrates the importance of taking control of your pace. Do not let perceived pressure or sometimes genuine pressure set a pace that is going to be detrimental to you and your team's mental health or physical presence in the improvement process. You know the track and rough distance to the finish line; you know that you and your team can run the distance. Listen to your body, not the clock. Listen to the people you are leading; if they are thriving and feeling fresh, step it up, just a little. If they are struggling and the pace is taking a toll, slow down and take your watch off for a little while to reset. You want those you are leading, and yourself as the leader, to enjoy the journey. Be present and have the time and head space to work through the fogginess. If you or your team are only focused on pace and competition, as in my running example, you will only be competing against yourselves, and the most likely result will be a negative impact on the culture and wellbeing of your community.

Kouzes and Posner (2012) argue that one thing that sustains a leader to consistently turn up, day after day, in a role with high levels of responsibility and accountability, long hours, and no shortages of challenges – and even with all the complexities in the role to still be able to get astonishing things achieved – is the concept of love. It is hard to imagine any leader who can sustain their energy, get people moving, and tackle the unexpected daily challenges that walk through the door, not loving what they are doing. You have the power to decide how you perceive your role. I continue to maintain that my role as a senior leader is hard work. It throws things at me that I have never encountered before. It is an emotional business, and therefore many people respond with their emotions before rationalising. This is difficult to manage at times. I could list the challenges that my role presents daily, weekly, monthly and yearly, and it would be a long list. The only list that I would consider longer is the list of rewards my leadership positions offer – the opportunities to influence an entire community in a way that will have an immeasurable impact on their future. Kouzes and Posner (2012) also argue that leaders must find their individual and unique voice, values, and a personal way to communicate and express their leadership philosophy. The SKIM Model is exactly that: a model or framework that will give you the platform to communicate your voice and style of leadership – one that will let you focus on your people, not on process.

The SKIM Model doesn't provide a set of capabilities that you need to effectively implement your leadership process and strategies; these are all covered in many different research papers on leadership, which may be found with a quick internet search. We have established the importance and impact of qualities such as optimism, enthusiasm, vision and a genuine positive intent towards every facet of the organisation you lead. What the SKIM Model does is give you the structure and provide the reason to "take your watch off" when you need to "listen to your body" (the people that you are leading) and a process that will support not just improvement but sustained, embedded improvement. After all, that is the ultimate leadership goal.

Dellaert and Davydov (2017) point out that effective leaders can harness and combine several high-level strategies that are logical, emotional and cooperative. Leaders are seen as politically savvy, create and maintain visibility, build and sustain personal trustworthiness, leverage networks, communicate and collaborate to build clarity, and motivate others. It is a complex position, and when you look at it from the perspective of capabilities, I can see why people often say, "You're a principal – wow, that must be a hard job!" They are right; it is difficult. However, I have the power to set up my structures and processes to ensure I have the technical management skills embedded, so I can focus on the people I lead. Improvement directly impacts and is measured within the people you are leading.

The final word

Kelpie Leadership Program

For several years, a principal colleague, Sam Irwin, and I have led a student leadership camp at a kelpie stud farm (Beloka Kelpie Stud – Welshpool, Victoria). The premise of the program is that our student leaders "adopt a kelpie" during the program and complete several mini-workshops and training opportunities, with the goal of becoming the kelpie's master for those few days. Ultimately, the test is the students' ability to coordinate their kelpies to successfully round up sheep. The kelpies have very different personalities: some are very compliant, some are a little cheeky, some will focus on their actual master (the kelpie's real trainer), and some are very stubborn. The program is structured with a series of opportunities for our students to conduct leadership reflections that must take place throughout the program. The consistent learnings of the young leaders have been mirrored from year to year, and every year listening to the students' reflections energises me – another item to add to the "why I love my role in leadership" list. Before I continue, I do need to acknowledge that we are talking about leading kelpies here, not people, so the skills and dispositions needed are different; however the message that the students take from their reflections are surprisingly common:

1. **If the kelpie is not following your instructions – it is not their fault.**
   Early on we often see a level of frustration when the student leader's adopted kelpie does not sit or stay or sometimes won't do anything that is instructed by the student. Throughout their workshop learning and training, students' opinions change to acknowledge that if their kelpie wasn't following their instructions, it was most likely because their kelpie did not understand what they were being asked to do. Often the communication was too wordy or not specific enough, or their verbal communication did not match their visual communication well enough for their kelpie to completely understand the instructions and hence follow the seemingly simple requests.

2. **Language is important.**
   Leading on from the communication challenge, the young leaders learn that they must use appropriate language that the kelpies both understand and can action. It is also imperative that their body language and arm movements match the language. The kelpies respond to known language and commands. They observe body language to decide how to respond. The disposition, body language and tone of the students is also highlighted as an area that may confuse the kelpie. These always have to be considered as the student communicates to ensure an effective understanding and result.

3. **Relationships are key.**

    The kelpies already have an owner, their normal trainer, so the young leaders must build a relationship with their kelpies so that there is a level of belief that this "new person" is going to be trustworthy and safe. Until this relationship is established, the kelpie will continue to look for their trusted leader for instructions.

There are a lot of other common reflections that our young leaders report; again we are talking about kelpies, but I will continue to argue that communication, language and relationships built on trust and genuine positive intent will build any leader's momentum. What a great lesson for aspiring leaders to learn early in their journey!

The SKIM Model is the vehicle that will allow you the cognitive time and space to focus on the greatest influence on your improvement agenda – your people. So now, as you are walking along the riverbank, you will be able to selectively pick up skimming stones and drop those that are not right for your organisation. You will be able to wait patiently for the right conditions, with the right stone. As you launch the stone, awaiting the first of many skims across the water's surface, you will have a level of confidence that, because you picked the right stone and had the right conditions, your skim will be effective and will sustain its pace until you reach the destination and your stone has finished its job. By that point, you will have already begun the search for your next perfect skimming stone.

References

Amabile, T., & Kramer, S. (2011). The power of small wins. *Harvard Business Review, 89*(5), 70-90.

Angelou, M. (1969). *I know why the caged bird sings.* Bantam Books.

AITSL (Australian Institute for Teaching and Leadership). (2017). Australian Institute for Teaching and School Leadership Standards. https://aitsl.edu.au

Barth, R. (2006). Improving relationships within the schoolhouse. *Educational Leadership: Improving Professional Practice, 63*(6), 8-13.

Breakspear, S., & Ryrie Jones, B. (2020). *Teaching sprints: How overloaded educators can keep getting better.* Corwin.

Cheliotes, L., & Reilly, M. (2010). *Coaching conversations: Transforming your school one conversation at a time.* Corwin.

Covey, S. (1989). *The 7 habits of highly effective people.* Simon and Schuster.

Defour, R. & Fullan, M. (2013). *Cultures built to last: Systemic PLCs at work.* Solution Tree Press.

Dellaert, M., & Davydov, S. (2017). *Influencing: The skill of persuasion, building commitment and getting results.* Centre for Creative Leadership.

Dinham, S. (2011). *How to get your school moving and improving.* Acer Press.

Elmore, R. (2004). *School reform from the inside out: Policy, practice, and performance.* Harvard Education Press.

Ezard, T. (2021). *Ferocious warmth: School leaders who inspire and transform.* Tracey Ezard.

Fisher, D., & Frey, N. (2013). *Engaging the adolescent learner: Gradual release of responsibility instructional framework.* IRA e-ssentials, 1-8.

Fullan, M. (2010). *Motion leadership: The skinny on becoming change savvy.* Corwin.

Fullan, M., & Quinn J. (2016). Coherence: The right drivers in action for schools, districts and systems. Corwin.

Gardner, J. (1993). *On leadership.* Free Press.

Goodwin, B. (2018). *Student learning that works: How brain science informs a student learning model.* McRel International.

Groysberg, B., & Slind, M. (2012). *Talk, Inc.: How trusted leaders use conversation to power their organisations.* Havard Business Review Press.

Guskey, T. (1983). Staff development and teacher change. *Educational Leadership, 41*(3), 57-60.

Hargreaves, A., & Fullan, M. (2012). *Professional capital: Transforming teaching in every school.* Routledge.

Hattie, J. (2012). *Visible learning for teachers: Maximising impact on learning.* Routledge Taylor & Francis Group.

Heifetz, R., & Linsky, M. (2002). *Leadership on the line: Staying alive through the dangers of leading.* Harvard Business School Press.

Knight, J. (2011). *Unmistakable impact: A partnership approach for dramatically improving instruction.* Corwin Press.

Knowles, M. S. (1968). Andragogy, not pedagogy. *Adult Learning, 16*(10), 350-52.

Kotter, J. P. (1996). *Leading change.* Harvard Business Review Press.

Kouzes, J., & Posner, B. (2012). *The leadership challenge: How to make extraordinary things happen in organisations.* Jossey-Bass.

Lencioni, P. (2006). If everything is important... The Table Group. https://www.tablegroup.com/if-everything-is-important/

Macklin, P., & Zbar, V. (2020). *Driving school improvement: Practical strategies and tools.* Acer Press.

Marzano, R., Warrick, P., & Simms, J. (2014). *A handbook for high reliability schools: The next steps in school reform.* Hawker Browlow Education & Marzano Research.

Maslow, A. (1966). *The psychology of science: A reconnaissance.* Harper Collins.

McCauley, C., & Van Velsor, E. (Eds.). (2004). *The Centre for Creative Leadership handbook of leadership development* (2nd ed.). Jossey-Bass.

McDonough, S., & Trotter, S. (2015). Promoting friendship through experiences in residential outdoor education. (Mini-thesis.)

McLagen, P. (2002). Success with change. *T+D, 56*(12), 44-53.

Munby, S. (2019). *Imperfect leadership: A book for leaders who know they don't know it all.* Crown House Publishing.

Munro, C., & Campbell, J. (2022). Coaching as a way of leading. *AEL 44*(4), 28-32.

National College for Teaching and Leadership. (2015). Lessons from Tim Brighthouse. NCTL.

NSW Department of Education. (2017). *Cognitive load theory practice guide.* Centre for Education Statistics and Evaluation.

Palmer, P. (1998). *The courage to teach: Exploring the inner landscape of a teacher's soul.* Jossey-Bass.

Parker, P. (2018). *The art of gathering: How we meet and why it matters.* Riverhead Books.

Prochaska, J. O., Velicer, W. F., Rossi, J. S., Goldstein, M. G., Marcus, B. H., Rakowski, W., Fiore, C., Harlow, L. L., Redding, C. A., Rosenbloom, D., & Rossi, S. R. (1994). Stages of change and decisional balance for 12 problem behaviors. *Health Psychology, 13*(1), 39-46. https://doi.org/10.1037/0278-6133.13.1.39

QELI. (2017). QELI leadership framework and behaviors of effective leaders.

Ratanjee, V. (2021). *Successful organisational change needs a strong narrative.* Gallup.

Robinson, V., Le Fevre, D., & Sinnema, C. (2016). *Open-to-learning leadership: How to build trust while tackling tough issues.* Hawker Brownlow Education.

Robinson, V. (2018). *Reduce change to increase improvement.* Corwin.

Rogers, E. (1962). *Diffusion of innovations.* Free Press of Glencoe.

Schwartz, B. (2004). *The paradox of choice: Why more is less.* Ecco.

Sharratt, L. (2019). *Clarity: What matters most is learning, teaching, and leading.* Corwin.

Shetty, J. (2020). *Think like a monk.* Thorsons.

Sinek, S. (2009). *Start with why: How great leaders inspire everyone to take action.* Portfolio.

Smith, I. (2005). Achieving readiness for organisational change. *Library Management, 26*(6/7), 408.

Sweller, J., Ayres, P., & Kalyuga, S. (2011). *Cognitive load theory.* Springer.

Walker, R., & Aritz, J. (2014). *Leadership talk: A discourse approach to leader emergence.* Business Expert Press.

Wehmeyer, M., & Zhao, Y. (2020). *Teaching students to become self-determined learners.* ASCD.

Wiliam, D. (2003). *Teacher quality: Why it matters and how to get more of it.* Institute of Education, University of London.

Wiliam, D. (2019). *Teaching not a research-based profession.* TES Magazine. https://www.tes.com/magazine/archive/dylan-wiliam-teaching-not-research-based-profession

www.ingramcontent.com/pod-product-compliance
Lightning Source LLC
Chambersburg PA
CBHW050418120526
44590CB00015B/2006